Eastern Birds of Prey

Eastern Birds of Prey

A Guide to the Private Lives of Eastern Raptors

Neal Clark

North Country Press • Unity, Maine

Special thanks to the Maine Department of Inland Fisheries and Wildlife, Massachusetts Audubon Society, and the Cornell Laboratory of Ornithology for their help in locating many of the photos for this book.

Library of Congress Cataloging in Publication Data

Clark, Neal, 1950-
    Eastern birds of prey.

    Bibliography: p.
    1. Birds of prey — United States.   I. Title.
QL696.F3C58   1983   598'.910974   83-4775
ISBN 0-945980-27-2 (formerly ISBN 0-89621-073-1 pbk.)

Cover photo by Dr. J. Kenneally.

Cover design by Abby Trudeau.

Book design by Tim Loeb.

fourth printing, 1990

To my parents,
who have always encouraged
my curiosity about the natural world.

Acknowledgments

The author gratefully thanks the following individuals and organizations who helped in various ways seeing this book through: Camp Chewonki in Wiscasset, Maine, where environmental ethics run deep, and where its long-time logo — the osprey — still hovers around The Point; Paul Roberts, editor of the *Bird Observer of Eastern Massachusetts,* who published my first article; John Thompson, who told me it was time to write a book; Mike Ricciuto, former editor of *New England Outdoors* magazine, who introduced me to Tim Loeb of Thorndike Press; the Harris Center for Conservation Education in Hancock, New Hampshire, my new rural home; Mt. Wachusett Animal Forest in Hubbardston, Massachusetts, for the freedom to photograph some of their raptors; the Appalachian Mountain Club, for allowing me to use portions of an article of mine that previously appeared in *Appalachia;* Doubleday and Co., for permission to quote from Neltje Blanchan's *Birds Worth Knowing;* Charles Scribner's Sons, for permission to quote from Michael Harwood's *View From Hawk Mountain,* used in the opening lines of my Introduction; and special thanks to Norman Boucher and Bruce Peck for their interest and support along the way.

Contents

PART II—NOCTURNAL RAPTORS

Introduction

"It was nothing to go up there with two or three boxes of shell and get rid of them. The hawks usually came in flocks. A fellow lived up there used to say they leave them out in bagsful, and when a flock came he says, 'Here comes another bagful.' " So recalls an old shooter concerning the goings-on at Hawk Mountain, Pennsylvania during the Roaring Twenties. Hunters held deep-seated grudges against all large birds, and traditionally hawks were just "vermin," "chicken hawks," "murderers," or "wanton killers," no good to anyone.

In the sharpshooter's eyes, all hawks were killers brandishing bloody claws who did in his poultry, game birds, and rabbits. The only good hawk was a dead one, and it didn't matter that they were formidable flyers or that they rid large areas of rodents; hawks still faced barrelfuls of shot while migrating low over the mountains. On some autumn days, upwards of 300 hunters would fire away at the passing birds above Kempton, Pennsylvania. Since hawks weren't edible, the bodies were not retrieved, and the wounded slowly perished while men sneered.

Between 1915 and 1951, Alaska paid bounties on more than 100,000 bald eagles — about ten times the number currently recorded in the Lower 48 — to protect salmon, when the real reason for the fish's decline was commercial overfishing. Snowy owls, as white and silent as falling snow, swept down from Canada to the Northeast in certain winters only to be shot for trophies. Even great horned owls, thought to take too many game birds, were blown away. And still are.

But mankind's violent relationship with birds of prey has tempered somewhat in the latter part of the 20th century. Hawk Mountain is now a sanctuary and hawk-watching hot spot; bald eagles are staging a slow comeback; owls and all other raptors have federal protection under the 1972 Migratory Bird Treaty.

Hawks, eagles, ospreys, vultures, and owls are known collectively as birds of prey, or raptors. They are all predators — creatures that kill other animals to survive. They hunt for meat, or, in some cases, insects, and are known for their strongly-hooked beaks and razor-sharp talons. Raptors, feared and maligned for centuries, are only now beginning to be understood. With DDT finally disappearing from the environment, the main threat today is loss of habitat. The National Wildlife Federation estimates that more than one million acres per year in this country are converted to roads and other forms of urban sprawl. The habitat destruction of today will prove harder to halt than the indiscriminant hunting of the past.

Sometimes it's difficult even for seasoned naturalists and scientists to be objective about predation. Few people enjoy seeing a goshawk decapitate a chipmunk, but predation is necessary in the web of life, and should be viewed from an overall population standpoint instead of an individual one. One of the rare cases where predator control of individual raptors seemed like a good idea occurred in the 1920s on Martha's Vineyard when hawks were shot to protect the few remaining heath hens. (The game bird became extinct, nonetheless, in

1932.) Predation may not be pretty but it is a biological necessity which tends to keep the ever-increasing populations of prey species in check before disease and starvation run rampant.

The purpose of this book is to enlighten and inform readers about the more common diurnal and nocturnal birds of prey found east of the Mississippi River. More than a field guide, this is a collection of background history, natural history, and anecdotes to be read before and immediately after a trip to the woods, and should especially come in handy once a bird has been identified. Species identification is but the first step toward becoming a complete birder and all-around naturalist. It is hoped that readers, upon finishing this book, will know more about raptor habits, and will appreciate and help protect them instead of despising them.

Ohio has the right idea; in 1981 the Ohio Audubon Council gave out bright orange signs to any landowner who'd post them. The signs, with a bird of prey on each, along with the words, "Don't Shoot," warn the uneducated that raptors are protected by state and federal laws. In addition to the signs, interested landowners receive brochures on the hawks and owls of Ohio. The same brochures are also distributed throughout the state's schools. With programs such as these, hawks and their kin might at long last be seen in their true light — aerial predators that are vital cogs in nature's intricate wheel on earth.

OSPREY

Photo by Kenneth W. Gardiner.

Chapter 1

OSPREY

Pandion haliaetus

Introductory Remarks

The cosmopolitan osprey, or fish hawk, is the only hawk-like bird that dives into the water. It is so well adapted to the fishing life that the species is found on every land mass on earth except New Zealand and Antarctica. Only a decade ago, however, it was in serious trouble, hovering near the brink of extinction.

There has been a gradual decline in the number of raptors and fish-eating birds dating back to the 1950s, due to persistent pesticides lingering in the environment. DDT, PCB, and other chlorinated hydrocarbons that do not readily dissolve in water, were removed from agricultural soils by evaporation or run-off, settling in the sea. There, marine organisms such as plankton, shrimp, and small fish concentrated these deadly compounds in large amounts, in turn to be consumed by pelagic birds like petrels and shearwaters. The osprey, a predator that feeds exclusively on fish, and is thus at the end of a long food chain, ingested the poisons in such quantities that it became an endangered species in several states.

The birds yielded fewer young during those high-chemical years, but, more importantly, there was an accompanying calcium carbonate deficiency experienced by females, making for thinner eggshells. As a result, many eggs broke under the weight of incubating adults. The renowned ornithologist, Roger Tory Peterson, noticed an alarming reduction in the number of active osprey nests near his Old Lyme, Connecticut home from 1956-1971: from 150 to about eight. In New Jersey during the 1940s, more than 500 osprey nests were recorded. By 1974 there were only 50.

Even more appalling, the largest known colony in the country (on Gardiners Island, off the tip of Long Island, New York) plummeted from 200 active nests to 100 between the years 1956-1960. This was immediately after a single spraying of DDT. Not until 1973 did the ospreys begin a comeback there. The 3,300-acre island is private property, and because there are ample fishing grounds nearby, coupled with the fact that no predatory mammals are present, ospreys have optimum breeding conditions. The birds were defenseless against the sole threat of toxic chemicals stored in their fat tissues.

DDT was banned in this country in 1972 because it was dangerous and obsolete. It killed predators but was not killing the insects as it once had (some 130 species of insects had become immune to it). As a direct result of the ban, the osprey has slowly returned from its rapid decline. Now, members of the New England Hawk Watch who cover the New Haven, Connecticut area can expect to view upwards of a thousand birds, where just a few years ago a couple hundred was the norm during the fall migration.

If people cared about individual nests like they do in Mattituck, N.Y., ospreys would be back for good. A pair of birds built a nest atop a tall third-base light tower on a baseball field. Relocation seemed imperative, so the local Nature Conservancy made a safe new site for them nearby — a wooden pallet on a utility pole stuck in the middle of the pond. While the ospreys were away, members quickly transferred the nest to the pallet with the use of a loaned cherry picker. Young were raised successfully, but the next April the adults started building over third base again. Three times the ill-placed nest had to be torn down until the birds settled in again at the pond.

Observation Guidelines

The osprey remains a threatened species in New England. It is an uncommon summer resident, frequenting the area from early April until early October, with Maine harboring the largest population. Most individuals winter in Florida or farther south, although some endure along the coast as far north as Long Island. Since it feeds exclusively on fish, the fish hawk is found only near water, be it lake, river, or ocean.

Standing almost two feet tall with a wingspan of up to six feet, this bird is our largest raptor next to the bald eagle, golden eagle, and turkey vulture. Because the vulture is not found in the same habitat as the osprey, only the eagle could be confused with it. The long, narrow wings of the osprey reveal distinct black patches at the wrist, which show well from below. Basically, the bird has a blackish back, white undersides, and a black cheek patch.

Ospreys can be differentiated from eagles by flight alone. When viewed from below, as is usually the case, ospreys have a noticeable bow or crook in the elbow areas which is diagnostic, i.e., the wings aren't extended to their limit except during migration. Ospreys flap a lot and often hover in place while hunting for live fish, and can look like large gulls from afar. They've been clocked migrating at 80 mph. Eagles, conversely, flap less and soar more, with their flat, wide wings fully extended. They are heavy fliers who rarely hover, and feed largely on *dead* fish.

Calls of the osprey are also distinctive; they are a series of loud, sharp, high-pitched whistles that sound like drawn-out chicken peepings. The excited calls carry well over water, and, one reason why farmers take to the bird, aside from them keeping hawks away, is that the screams serve as a warning in the same way a watch dog's growls do when a stranger approaches.

Natural History

This aquatic hunter feasts entirely on fish that swim close to the surface, including herring, hornpout, trout, flying fish, carp, menhaden, perch, pike, pickerel, and salmon. It is well adapted to catching them, as evidenced by the soles of the feet, which sport spiny projections called spicules that firmly grasp the slippery, wriggling prey.

The method of hunting, surely the most primitive form of fishing, is a marvel to witness. A bird, flying perhaps a hundred feet above the water, will spot some rippling movement far below, hover heavily for a minute, then fold in its wings and swoop down at an angle, as if it were to land like a duck. Talons-first it hits the blue with a big splash, wings up and head down. Seizing a fish in its claws, it struggles up out of the water, shaking itself off, and heads for a favorite perch to pick apart the catch.

Fish are usually carried away headfirst because they are caught that way (from the rear), but, if not, they are turned around in the air. Fish up to five pounds are reported to have been caught. A curious habit often observed is foot-washing. A bird will glide low over the water, almost touching the surface, and then dip and drag its feet for ten or fifteen yards. This practice apparently removes fish slime accumulated on the talons.

Nesting sites vary greatly, from the ground to 60 feet up in a dead tree, on utility poles, fishing shacks, aerials, billboards, windmills, and even chimneys. On the Sheepscot River, near Wiscasset, Maine, two pairs of seaworthy ospreys have chosen lighted channel buoys to build upon the last few years. The U.S. Coast Guard cooperates by setting out duplicate buoys for the summer season.

Nest foundations are composed of sticks up to four feet long and three inches in diameter, mixed with sod. The lining is usually grass, bark, or vines, but an assortment of odd materials has also been found inside: shirts, shoes, rope, fishnets, fishlines, hats, dolls, bottles, sponges, etc. Since the nest is used by the same pair year after year, it grows with each additional twig, and a majority of old nests show grass growing amid large mats of sod and cow dung. Sometimes nests reach eight feet high and may be used consecutively for 30 years before the supporting tree, often long-dead, collapses under the weight.

Two to four eggs are laid in May, followed by a month's incubation by the female. The young stay home for about two months, during which time the following procedure can be observed: the male, grasping a fish, drops onto the nest and tears the food into half-inch pieces, gives them to his mate bit by bit, who then chews some more and feeds the young.

While the nestlings are still downy, hot summer temperatures can make them uncomfortable, panting like dogs, so the female stands overhead with wings out to shield them. By the time they're six weeks old, the parents drop whole fish into the nest, and the nestlings feed themselves without fighting. Instinctively they soon learn to fish on their own.

The osprey is a peaceable, if not accommodating, neighbor with most other species; there are many accounts of house sparrows, starlings, or grackles living in the lower sections of a huge osprey nest. But the species has a torrid history with bald eagles, who often rob ospreys of their catch in mid-air. And crows suck the eggs dry whenever they get the chance. Over all, though, it's *Homo sapiens* that has the direct influence on whether or not the osprey attains its 20-year lifespan. DDT may be gradually vanishing, but so too are prime fishing grounds.

GOSHAWK   Photo courtesy of Cornell Laboratory of Ornithology.

Chapter 2

NORTHERN GOSHAWK

Accipiter gentilis

Introductory Remarks

Accipiters are hawks sporting short, rounded wings and long tails that facilitate easy cruising through dense woodlands. Also known as bird hawks, accipiters are quick and low-flying, and the goshawk, or blue darter, is the largest family member in North America.

Goshawks and other raptors were trained (and still are) to chase either prey or lures for the sport of falconry, which dates to 700 B.C. It reached its height of popularity around 1500 A.D. in Europe, and by 1750, due to the increased use of firearms in hunting, falconry was largely a forgotten art. Although there are fewer than 2,000 licensed, practicing falconers in the U.S. today, the sport is coming back.

Robert Arbib, editor of the National Audubon Society's *American Birds,* said that legalizing falconry is equivalent to "legalizing rape," while Aldo Leopold, the father of modern wildlife management, saw it as a "high form of recreation and a perfect hobby." Perhaps the most objective view comes from the Bureau of Sport Fisheries and Wildlife: "Individual falconers may be expected to contribute importantly to the collection of population data, development of captive propagation techniques, and to assist wildlife agencies with the restoration of endangered or locally expired raptor species."

The sport is regulated by federal and state agencies; every falconer must pass a written test, and new falconers go through a two-year apprenticeship program, as well as an inspection of hawk houses and equipment before being issued a license. Because adult birds prove hard to train, nestlings or those caught near the nest soon after fledging are used. The formerly abundant peregrine falcon was the favored species, but with its demise, the goshawk now reigns as the royal flusher in the East.

"Of the dozen or so species of hawks and falcons currently available to falconers in the eastern U.S.," reports Chuck Keene, director of the Museum of the Hudson Highlands in New York, "the goshawk is to falconry what the Labrador is to retrieving. The gos, with its long, beautiful tail for a rudder, can 'thread the needle' through those maples, and overtake blacks and mallards in a flash."

Besides being put to use by man, goshawks are also put to death because they eat other birds, including poultry and game. Until the 1970s, bounties of $5 or more were paid in many states. Pompous, man-centered attitudes prevailed even in the ornithological community, as evidenced by the remarks of the reputable Arthur Cleveland Bent: "He is cordially hated, and justly so, by the farmer and sportsman, and for his many sins he often pays the extreme penalty." Edward Forbush, the first State Ornithologist of Massachusetts, wrote of the goshawk back in 1927, "Its attack is swift, furious, and deadly. In the death grapple it clings ferociously to its victim, careless of its own safety until the unfortunate creature succumbs to its steely grip. Its stroke is terrible."

Hatred for the blue darter was based mainly on fear — fear of losing one's livelihood, or fear of personal injury. There is an authenticated report from Connecticut of a bird that chased a hen into a kitchen and killed it in front of two people (the hawk was subsequently clubbed with a cane). Another report, from Lambert Lake, Maine, told of a harried hen escaping from a goshawk by run-

GOSHAWK   Photo by William S. Clark.

ning under a woman's skirt (the hawk pursued until it was trampled). Even in the environmentally enlightened 1980s, the goshawk is resented — even loathed — like a desperado. No other hawk in the East is as notorious nor as persecuted. As a living thing, a skilled hunter, it deserves respect.

Observation Guidelines

Unlike predators such as the osprey and peregrine, who feed at the top of the food chain and thus take in toxic chemicals via poisoned fish and birds, respectively, the goshawk has actually benefitted by mankind since the 1940s. It feeds lower on the food chain (mammals and game birds, etc.), thereby escaping most chemical poisoning. In addition, and more importantly, there's been a gradual spread in New England of mature forest land, which is its prime habitat. New Hampshire, for example, has gone from 20% to 80% woodland in the past century due to the disuse of farms.

The goshawk remains, however, an uncommon breeder in New England. It has bred as far south as Maryland, and is extending its range in that direction, but the best seasons to spot it are fall and winter. Every nine or ten years, when there is a marked decline in either hare or grouse populations in Canada, goshawks come pouring down for better pickings. Beginning in October, they move southward, but even then they aren't that common; in 1980 the Hawk Migration Association of North America recorded only 28 birds from various watches in Maine. New Hampshire and Vermont each recorded 17 individuals during the same fall migration. By comparison, 2,540 sharp-shinned hawks, another accipiter, were recorded on the same watch. Numbers can, however, be deceiving. The sharp-shinned hawk itself is breeding less frequently in settled areas south of Canada, while the goshawk is holding its own.

Likely habitats to check for goshawks in winter are farmlands (much to the chagrin of chicken-breeders), open country and woodland edges. City dumps are also places to look, for these sites produce rats that hungry hawks can easily snatch up. During the breeding season they prefer more remote coniferous forests.

The goshawk is slightly larger than a crow, with a wingspan of three and a half feet. Its back is gray, the front a barred, paler gray. In all plumages it shows a broad white eye-stripe, and at extremely close range, fiery red eyes glow.

It can be distinguished from our other two accipiters (the sharp-shinned and Cooper's hawks) most readily by flight and calls. The goshawk has a much slower wingbeat than either of the other two, thus adhering to the old birders' rule of thumb: the larger the bird, the slower it flaps. While migrating it flies high and steadily, rarely soaring. While hunting, however, it flies low, darting about deep woods.

Jack Swedberg, photographer for the Division of Fisheries and Wildlife in Massachusetts, knows all too well how it flies, for he was almost scalped by one a few years ago. "Usually a goshawk will veer at the last moment," he reported, "and just miss, but this one didn't. She grew more aggressive during the days I was photographing her and during that single spring she stole twelve caps off my head. There was one occasion when she really let me have it. She came in and sank her talons into my forehead. She hit me so hard — she was coming at me around 60 miles an hour and weighed probably two pounds — that she knocked me off my feet." One of the shots he managed to get shows the bird hurtling right at him (and the viewer) talons first. One almost gets the impulse to duck when first glancing at the photograph.

Goshawks are silent except during the breeding season. The excited calls about the nest are long series of rapid, shrill notes: Keh-keh-keh-keh-keh! They sound vaguely like a herring gull's calls, although faster and not as gutteral. People who accidentally trespass into their nesting sanctums know they've gone too far when the unnerving notes suddenly shoot out of the woods, bouncing off trees and piercing the ears. The perceptive person heeds the warnings and skirts the area.

Natural History

In a study done by Heinz Meng in Ithaca, New York, it was shown that goshawks preyed mainly on red squirrels and crows during spring and summer. Gray squirrels, cottontails, chipmunks, and grouse were also taken. During winter especially, when more of these hawks are around, poultry is also taken, including chickens, guinea fowl, and domestic ducks and pigeons.

The usual method of hunting is by overtaking the prey bird with its strong flight. When a goshawk nears its prey, it closes the wings, pushes the feet forward, and strikes the victim, driving in the stiletto-sharp talons. A different method is sometimes employed when the hawk goes after hares or rabbits; then it follows snowy tracks by walking and hopping like a crow, sometimes surprising a dozing hare en route. This terrestrial stalking behavior is used only in tangled undergrowth, where wings are useless.

The goshawk is a formidable predator, as Edward Forbush found out while shooting some jays one day: "I had shot three or four when I noticed that not one had reached the ground. Shooting another, I watched it fall, when a goshawk swept out from the trees into the very smoke from my gun and snatched it from the air."

Prey larger than the hawk itself, such as some breeds of poultry, can be killed and consumed in two or three meals. The blue darter starts the feast by ripping off the head and legs. Other than plucking out bird feathers, nothing is wasted, and the indigestible matter (bone, fur, hair, etc.) is ejected from the crop through the mouth as a two-inch, matted pellet. These pellets, or castings, are accurate indicators of diet.

Accounts of nesting goshawks attacking humans are legion. As soon as anyone gets within a few hundred yards of a nesting pair, the racket begins, followed by strafing if the warning calls aren't heeded. Only the foolhardy try to approach a nest tree.

Dr. George Sutton told of a hair-raising experience many years ago in Pennsylvania: "I crawled into a rudely constructed blind where I crouched motionless, hoping that I would not be detected by the hawks. The female bird drove the departing men to the edge of the woods and then returned, calmer for an instant or two, and then, spying me without the slightest difficulty, redoubled her fury and bore down upon me with savage intent. Intrepid and insistent, she swooped at me from all directions and only the branches of the blind kept me from the blows of her feet, although the protecting boughs cracked and snapped at each onslaught. My being alone doubtless increased her daring and she perched at a distance of only twelve feet and screamed in my face, her bright eyes glaring, and her powerful beak expectantly parted."

Preferred nesting sites are in deep woods, often in a bowl area surrounded by hills. The nest is placed up to 50 feet high near the trunk of a tall tree — usually deciduous, such as a beech, birch, or maple. It's a bulky affair three feet across, made of sticks, and lined with hemlock bark and greens. Breeding pairs return year after year to the same locale if not the same nest.

Three or four oval, pale blue eggs are laid in early April in southern New England, late April-early May in northern sections. Females do most of the incubating, which takes about a month, and the young fledge in the same amount of time. During the rearing period, adult birds sometimes utter a slower Caw-caw-caw! when approaching the young with food. This cawing is rarely heard because the adults don't usually feed the nestlings while intruders are present.

The late naturalist, Edwin Way Teale, noticed one winter at his Hampton, Connecticut home that a few days after a single goshawk appeared, the number of blue jays in the area dropped in half. And, of 160+ mourning doves that fed daily in his driveway, only four remained. The rest fled until spring; such is the kind of respect commanded by the bold one.

Regardless of how bold the goshawk can be, it is spiritless towards its major juggernaut — habitat destruction — and birds quickly abandon their nests when adjacent woodlots shrink before their eyes. As they push southward on tentative wings, seeking new breeding territories, they'll find sufficient food. The only uncertainty is: will there be enough standing timber to shelter them in the decades to come?

IMMATURE SHARP-SHINNED HAWK   Photo © by Leonard Lee Rue III.

Chapter 3

SHARP-SHINNED HAWK

Accipiter striatus

Introductory Remarks

The sharp-shinned, or bullet hawk, is the only accipiter with a long square tail. A "bird hawk," it too was scorned as mere vermin, and killed at every opportunity. Even so-called birdlovers, the likes of author Neltje Blanchan, had definite prejudices against the little sharpie. "Unhappily," she wrote in 1917, "it is perhaps the most common hawk in the greater part of the United States, and therefore does more harm than all the others. It is mentioned as a bird worth knowing only because everyone should be able to distinguish friend from foe. Let the guns be turned towards these bloodthirsty, audacious miscreants, and away from the red-tailed and red-shouldered species, beneficent, majestic kings of the air!" How times and attitudes have changed; any birder making similar comments today would be immediately ostracized from all birding circles and be forced to hang up the binoculars.

If birders such as Blanchan turned their noses up at the sharp-shinned hawk, imagine what the farmers and sportsmen felt. Example: A farmer once bragged about bagging 56 while sitting in a chair on his front lawn near Point Pelee, Ontario. Dr. Ditmer Stone, former *Auk* editor, said that in one week in 1920, 1,400 were shot for food by gunners at Cape May, New Jersey. And Roger Tory Peterson saw, in 1935, 800 of these hawks trying to fly across a road one morning in the same town. By noon 254 lay dead on the pavement.

Observation Guidelines

The National Audubon Society's 1982 "Blue List," an early warning list of diminishing bird species, included the sharp-shin. It is considered endangered in Ontario. In New England it's an uncommon-to-rare breeder. The hurricane of Sept. 21, 1938, greatly contributed to the overall decline of the species, for scores of known nesting sites were razed during that infamous storm. The species has not yet fully recovered. Only during migration can large numbers still be seen, and at such times, in late September, they usually rank second to the thousands of broad-winged hawks recorded.

This jay-sized accipiter is found in coniferous and deciduous forests, but while migrating or wintering it can be seen almost anywhere, including the seashore. Adults have a slate-gray back and a rusty, barred breast. Because small Cooper's hawks can be identical in size and appearance to the sharp-shinned hawk, the only sure way to tell them apart is by the tail. The sharpie has a square tail, the Cooper's is rounded. Females of both species are considerably *larger* than the males, a trait generally true of all birds of prey.

It flies with a flap, flap, flap and a sail, but rarely soars for extended periods except while migrating. On such occasions, if windy, individuals tuck their wingtips against their flanks, thus creating a tear-drop shape that really gets them cruising. They also use this maneuver when playfully divebombing other hawks who crowd their air space. Overall, it is a quick, agile, buoyant flyer.

The calls are series of very rapid cackles, given when the bird is alarmed. They have a slight nasal quality to them, and are more musical and less clipped than the kestrel's calls.

Natural History

The sex of a bird, strangely, affects the sharp-shin's diet. In a study conducted in 1966, R.W. Storer found that male birds, which averaged 100 grams, ate birds about 18 grams in weight, while females, which averaged 170 grams, ate birds about 28 grams in weight. Preyed birds constitute fully 90% of their diet, the rest of the menu being mice, insects, bats, etc. They have been known to go after birds larger than themselves, including screech owls, night herons, and quail, and they'll even crash into windows trying to reach caged birds.

When lean times come, especially on migration, they sometimes turn on themselves. Tom Smylie, a biologist with the U.S. Fish and Wildlife Service, said, "We do know that something occasionally goes wrong and they run out of prey, and some will turn cannibalistic. Down in the Tortugas, I've seen these migrating birds dying of apparent starvation, and I've seen them attack other sharp-shinned hawks that we'd trapped in mist nets for banding."

The main method of hunting is pouncing from trees or bushes onto the startled prey. The vegetation helps hide the waiting hawk as well as mask the approach. At other times the hawk makes low sallies from perch to perch on the chance that something will be flushed. Captured birds are immediately and rapidly plucked with an efficient beak. Clumps of bloodied feathers are torn out and cast to the winds in one savage motion. After it's been denuded, the whole carcass is devoured, bones and all.

Individual birds vary in their reactions to human intruders; some slip off their nests and retreat, while others attack. Henry Rust underestimated the danger he was in while climbing a nest tree: "The male struck one hard rap between my shoulders while I was examining the young, and the female kept striking so close to my head as to make it very uncomfortable. After descending to the ground I hid near a small fir tree to watch the old birds. Shortly afterwards the female made a swoop direct from the nest and just grazed my head. I moved out of the thicket and both birds followed, perching eight or ten feet from me, uttering their shrill cries, and darting at my head at short intervals."

Courtship starts in April, with pairs peeping to each other like barnyard chicks. Both sexes flutter their wings, and the males whine, followed by repeated matings that last about 30 seconds each. During this season the males vigorously defend the breeding territory, which can be hundreds of acres in size.

Preferred nesting sites are in coniferous woods and groves containing white pine, spruce, or hemlock. The nest may be on a branch or in a crotch 30-40 feet high, and is huge (two feet in diameter) considering the size of the bird. (Same-sized blue jays build nests with eight-inch diameters — one-third the sharp-shin's.) Because of the bulkiness of the nest and its placement high in trees, incubating birds are difficult to spot from below. Nests are composed of twigs, and lined with pine bark or, rarely, grass and moss.

In Massachusetts, eggs are laid early in May, and in northern New England, late May. Four or five spherical eggs are produced on alternate days, and incubation takes three weeks with both mates participating. Especially after incubation begins, one can find feathers and wings of small prey birds nearby.

The eggs, pale-blue or white with chocolate-brown blotches that form wreaths at either end, are the prettiest of all hawk eggs. Because of this, they were highly prized by oologists, or egg collectors. In the nineteenth century and the early part of this century, the science of oology was a popular offshoot of ornithology. Much of the collecting was for scientific purposes, but when everyone got into the act, including eager boys, the thievery only served to enlarge personal collections and deplete the birds' clutches. Sometimes collectors robbed eggs just to see how many the females would lay; in 1882, Calvin Rawson bragged of taking 18 sharp-shinned eggs from a nest in one season.

Egg collectors would drill a hole into the side of an egg, insert a blowpipe, and blow the contents out. If an embryo were inside, a larger hole had to be drilled so an embryo hook could be used. Today, raptor eggs are relatively safe from the greedy hands of these pseudo-scientists. Oology is still a science, but the practice of collecting eggs solely to outdo the competition is long dead. It's also against the law. No protected species can be tampered with at *any* stage of development.

The young sharp-shins remain in the nest for a month or more, during which time they make the parents forage even more than usual, since each hawklet can consume three small birds in a day. If the staple bird diet is depleted, adults scrounge for items such as locusts, cicadas, and large beetles.

At Walden Pond on July 21, 1858, according to Henry David Thoreau's journal, he found an active sharp-shin nest: "Saw several of the young flitting about and occasionally an old bird. The nest was in a middling-sized white pine, some twenty feet from the ground, resting on two limbs close to the main stem. It was quite solid, composed entirely of twigs about as big round as a pipe-stem or less; was some fifteen inches in diameter and one inch deep, or nearly flat, and perhaps five inches thick. It was very much dirtied on the sides by the droppings of the young. As we were standing about the tree, we heard again the note of a young one approaching. We dropped upon the ground, and it alighted on the edge of the nest; another alighted nearby, and a third a little further off. The young were apparently as big as the old, but still lingered about the nest and returned to it. I could hear them coming some distance off. Their note was a kind of peeping squeal, which you might at first suspect to be made by a jay; not very loud, but as if to attract the old and reveal their whereabouts. The note of the old bird which occasionally dashed past, was somewhat like that of the marsh hawk or pigeon woodpecker, a cackling or clattering sound, chiding us. The old bird was anxious about her inexperienced young, and was trying to get them off. At length she dashed close past us, and appeared to fairly strike one of the young, knocking him off his perch, and he soon followed her off. I saw the remains of several birds lying about in that neighborhood, and saw and heard again the young and old thereabouts for several days after."

Although the sharp-shinned hawk breeds less frequently in New England now, healthy numbers can still be seen migrating in September and October. On windy days they fly low enough over mountains and in and out of brush that binoculars aren't needed. Besides, there's no time to focus.

Many years ago, two ornithologists stood at Point Pelee, Ontario counting sharp-shins passing overhead. In a half-hour 207 were counted. Today, as evidenced by a count made in the New Haven, Connecticut area, birders can witness the same spectacle. On October 14, 1979, 3,800 were recorded. Watching the numbers of them migrating is impressive, but even more stimulating is seeing one of the little cutthroats up close as it careens through an eastern forest, hounding hapless songbirds.

COOPER'S HAWK

Photo by Richard Borden.

Chapter 4

COOPER'S HAWK

Accipiter cooperii

Introductory Remarks

The Cooper's hawk, which is basically a larger version of the sharp-shinned, is the only medium-sized accipiter with a rounded tail. Some individual birds are almost the size of a crow.

In the 1930s, Cooper's hawks accounted for three per cent of the total number of raptors counted at Hawk Mountain Sanctuary in Pennsylvania, but since 1960 they have usually accounted for less than one per cent. DDT and other pesticides have decimated this species, and although DDT was banned in the U.S. in 1972, and Dieldrin two years later, the hawk is still struggling to regain its former status. The fact that it is a migratory bird clouds the future; many individuals winter as far south as Mexico and Central America, where liberal doses of those chemicals are still being applied to crops. Cooper's hawks don't ingest the poisons directly, but rather indirectly — through poisoned birds they eat.

In Costa Rica and other countries, farmers don't even know what they're spraying the cotton, coffee, and bananas with. It can be DDT, Dieldrin, Endrin, and other hard pesticides, which are applied as often as 28 times in a growing season because the insects are becoming so pesticide-resistant. Sometimes more than 700 human poison cases are reported during a three-month period.

The United States and Western Europe continue to manufacture dangerous pesticides, including DDT, for export to Third World countries despite the fact that they are banned from use in *this* country. The control of these unsafe products is slow in coming because of resistance by governments and lobbying by corporations to block new regulations. Obviously it's a world-wide health issue concerning humans and wildlife alike, and one not easily resolved.

Helen and Noel Snyder studied the Cooper's hawk in the early 1970s and found thin eggshells and reproductive failure, especially in the East. The Snyders believe the reason for eastern populations suffering so much is that eastern birds prey 80 to 90 per cent upon small birds, while in the Southwest half the birds' diet consists of small mammals and lizards, which are less affected by chemicals. In California, the Cooper's hawk is doing well, and falconry is apparently not a threat there.

Observation Guidelines

The Cooper's hawk is a threatened species in this country, which is not as serious as endangered, but it's a rare and local breeder throughout its range. It breeds as far north as Lake Superior over to central Maine, and is a permanent resident from southern New England down to Florida. In some areas, particularly the northern limits of eastern deciduous forests, the goshawk is supplanting it.

Birds are on their breeding grounds from April through September, with the heaviest migratory flights occuring in mid-October as the hawks synchronize their departure with that of their prey. This is a hawk of broken deciduous and coniferous woods, and along with the sharp-shinned hawk, it shows a preference for white pine groves.

The Cooper's hawk is one of the most difficult hawks to positively identify, but expert birders look for a fairly big accipiter with a long, rounded tail, and a wingspan of approximately two feet. The tail, if

COOPER'S HAWK (detail)   Photo by Richard Borden.

seen clearly, is diagnostic. Cooper's hawks appear longer-headed, show a slower wingbeat than sharp-shins, and also soar more. Calls are high, piercing series of notes suggesting a flicker or hairy woodpecker in distress. These alarm notes are generally emitted only near the nest.

Natural History

Roy Gerig, of Salem, Oregon witnessed a bizarre method of killing prey in 1978. He saw a Cooper's hawk *drown* a starling. "Once in the water with the starling," he reported, "the hawk merely stood on top of it, and when the starling would struggle to raise its head and a wing out of the water, the hawk would shift its feet so that it pushed the starling's head back under the surface. The hawk appeared to be nervous with me standing only about thirty feet away, but made no attempt to leave for about four or five minutes, by which time the starling had stopped struggling entirely and appeared to be dead. Then the hawk flew easily away, the starling in its grasp." Gerig also managed to take some satisfactory photographs for *American Birds*. Whether this incident is an example of intelligence or just instinct, no one knows, but it is a fascinating example of adaptive behavior.

Heinz Meng found in Ithaca, New York, that Cooper's hawks fed 82 percent on birds — mainly starlings. They're also terribly fond of chickens. If there *is* such a bird as a "chicken hawk," this is it. They probably take more chickens and domestic pigeons than most other hawks combined, but because they don't soar, they're not easy targets. Instead, of soaring buteos take the brunt of the farmers' wrath.

Dr. Albert Fisher, who worked for the Bureau of Biological Survey at the turn of the century (the forerunner of the U.S. Fish and Wildlife Service, begun in 1940), and peered into more avian stomachs than anyone else, wrote on the Cooper's hawk: "Of 133 stomachs examined, 34 contained poultry or game birds; 52, other birds; 11, mammals; 1, frog; 3, lizards; 2, insects; and 39 were empty." Mammals commonly taken include hares and rabbits, opossums, squirrels, rats, and mice.

The Cooper's hawk is a crafty hunter and was bold as Robin Hood; Dr. Fisher once told of a bird that attacked a rock-collecting friend without provocation. After several attacks, the hawk was finally dispatched with the geologist's hammer. There are also many accounts of these daredevils flying in and out of barns and around people, bent on reaching their prey.

At home, the Cooper's hawk is usually more subdued, although once the eggs are hatched, some birds still feel the urge to strike. Because the hawk hunts away from the nesting area, customary prey such as songbirds can be found thriving safely in the immediate vicinity. The hawk's favorite nesting site is in a white pine grove, but deciduous and mixed woods containing ample oaks were also chosen.

Both sexes help build the two-foot wide nest, alternating their half-minute visits to allow for working room, while the other mate either stands guard or searches for more materials. The nest, composed of sticks and twigs, and lined with pine or oak bark, is placed in a crotch from 30 to 60 feet up.

Four or five bluish white eggs (often spotted with brown) are laid in late April south of New England, or in May in northern regions. The female does most of the incubating, which takes a little less than a month. Young birds prove to be hearty eaters; Dr. Harry Roddy reported in *The Auk* in 1888 a six-week-old bird that averaged eight sparrows and a house mouse daily. A neighbor, who didn't know it was a pet, shot it a month later, thus ending the experiment.

With the advent of large, multi-floored chicken buildings, attacks on poultry have decreased over the years, but Cooper's hawks haven't lost their taste. Safer chicken houses result in happier farmers, and the hawks are forced to keep their hunting skills honed, instead of dulling them on stupid fowl.

RED-TAILED HAWK

Chapter 5

RED-TAILED HAWK

Buteo jamaicensis

Introductory Remarks

The red-tailed hawk is the only buteo in our range with a red tail. Members of this genus show broad wings, short, fan-shaped tails, and often circle high in the sky. They also hunt from perches.

Although the redtail prefers small rodents, it takes a chicken on occasion, and, because it soars, makes an easy target. Hundreds were shot for sport at Hawk Mountain, Pennsylvania, before it became a sanctuary, and sometimes a wounded bird was suspended by a string from a branch to lure others within shotgun range. This so-called hen hawk of bygone days has taken everything the farmers and gunners could fire at it, and flown away unruffled. Today a truce has been called. The redtail is now viewed as an ally of man, which it has been all along; it just took mankind many years to understand.

Observation Guidelines

Partly because of this unwritten truce, it is a common hawk — more so now than 50 years ago — and one ornithologist estimated that they number about a million, making it one of North America's most common raptors. It is a permanent resident throughout most of the United States. Breeding birds north of Lake Ontario migrate in October as far south as Panama, accounting for 18 to 20 per cent of all raptors seen on Northeast hawk watches.

As the species is so abundant and likely to come into contact with humans, a few words about care for sick or wounded birds seems appropriate: The North American Falconry Association recommends that any raptor in trouble be wrapped in a towel with its head hooded and legs tied. (Raptors do not move in the dark.) Get the bird immediately to a veterinarian or a treatment facility, making sure it doesn't suffocate en route, as birds are highly susceptible to overheating.

Raptors held overnight should never be put in a cage, for they tend to beat themselves on the wires. Instead, a large cardboard box or an empty room with all windows covered is better. Feed the bird road-killed rodents or birds, or other fresh, raw meat. After the patient has recovered from the shock of the accident and capture, which may take a day, the chances are it'll feed. Anyone who is inexperienced at raptor care and rehabilitation should get the bird to a qualified handler as soon as possible.

Migrating adults seen from above can be identified by the rufous tail, which is pale underneath. Immature birds are not as richly colored, but both stages reveal a light breast and a dark, streaked belly. They sometimes hover above open country or dry woodlands in search of prey, and are found in the very same areas as great horned owls — the hawks hunting by day, the owls by night. Redtails are also seen perched within a few yards of busy highways, looking for live prey or roadkills. Observant motorists can sometimes spot one every few miles by looking for the contrasting belly band up in a sentinel tree.

Calls are actually cries — long, drawn-out, raspy screams that sound something like Kee-ahh-r-r! Birds frequently call while soaring, thus attracting other raptors. The redtail has little to fear, however, as it's the largest hawk likely to be patrolling the airways.

IMMATURE RED-TAILED HAWK   Photo © by Leonard Lee Rue III.

Natural History

Approximately 85% of the redtail diet consists of rodents and other small mammals, the rest being reptiles, amphibians, and some poultry and game birds. They've also been known to eat skunks, raccoons, woodchucks, muskrats, and bats, but some of these items are undoubtedly in the form of carrion, which they settle for in lean times.

Laboratory tests by Joan Dobbs at the University of California-Davis in 1978 determined that color, size, and texture of food are all important factors influencing food acceptance by red-tailed hawks. She and her associates, using artificially colored chick carcasses, found that the hawks chose yellow over blue, green, or red. Mice weighing under 7.5 grams were swallowed whole, while anything larger was torn apart before being eaten.

The two major methods of hunting are soaring with a sharp eye downward, and perching for hours in a dead or live tree, watching for the slightest movement. Sometimes, while stalking a squirrel or chipmunk, they hunt in pairs — one on each side of a tree. When reduced to chasing grasshoppers, they do so by hovering and hopping, snatching up the insects while barely touching down.

Their amazing power of vision is demonstrated in this old account from Dr. Benjamin Warren in Pennsylvania: "I saw a redtail circling over the meadows; every circle took him higher and higher in the air, until at an altitude where he appeared no larger than a blackbird, he stopped, and with nearly closed wings, descended like an arrow to a tree near by me; from this perch, almost the same instant he had alighted, he flew to the ground and snatched from its grassy covert a mouse. The momentum with which this bird passed through the atmosphere produced a sound not very unlike that of the rush of distant water."

The redtail is generally shy and unaggressive toward people. Few birds stay to defend the nest, and assaults are rare. Massachusetts birder Paul Roberts went eyeball to eyeball with a charging bird once. "I was hawkwatching," he remembers, "on a small mountain in late September. There was not much activity, so I put down my spotting scope and set up an owl decoy I had brought with me to attract migrating sharp-shinned hawks. I placed the paper-mache decoy high on a stick in a shrub and turned to walk back to my observation post. Suddenly, directly in front of me, seemingly only a few yards away, was an immature red-tailed hawk gliding at me head-on. It gave its wild, raspy kree-e-e-e call, now familiar to so many people because of the Buick commercials on television. I wheeled and ducked quickly to avoid the hawk, knocking my scope to the rocks. As I turned to watch the hawk fly away, I understood what had happened. The hawk had not been coming at me but at that paper-mache great horned owl. I had merely been standing directly in front of the decoy. The sight and sound of a large, wild raptor swooping down on me (the owl) was well worth the dents to the telescope."

Toward other birds, redtails are largely indifferent. Should a hawk be mobbed by crows (which is often the case with all raptors), it tries to avoid the pecking, but if the assault gets out of hand, it will flip over in the air on its back to show its talons. Many crows, blackbirds, and kingbirds are killed when they carry their harassing too far.

Paired redtails display courtship behavior throughout the spring, even after the young are born. Eustace Sumner, Jr., wrote about their aerial displays: "About ten times, while they were circling near together, the male would lower his legs and adjust his circles so that he came above his mate, and about four times he actually touched her back.''

A majority of eastern nests are placed 30 to 70 feet up in an oak tree, especially red oak. Dry woodlands with white pines are heavily used, and birds sometimes build on the edges of small tracts quite close to civilization; a pair successfully raised young for three consecutive years within a hundred yards of a Cramer Electronics plant near Needham, Massachusetts. Nests are well made of sticks, and lined with bark, moss, or greens. The green sprigs are continually renewed for the duration of incubation.

After the flat nest is built by both mates, two or three eggs are laid and incubated by the female for a month. The male feeds the female while she's sitting. Egg dates range from early March in Florida to early April in Massachusetts. The young birds remain in the nest for at least four weeks, the last two being spent practicing wing movements prior to fledging. Although some individuals attain fifteen years, only one out of four will survive to breed.

Anyone who seldom looks up will still spot the common red-tailed hawk endlessly circling on invisible thermals, rising higher towards the clouds, until it passes out of sight. Binoculars cannot bring it back. Is it still hunting or just loafing up there? No one knows, but the view of the countryside must be magnificent.

BROAD-WINGED HAWK

Photo © by Leonard Lee Rue III.

Chapter 6

BROAD-WINGED HAWK

Buteo platypterus

Introductory Remarks
This buteo, barely the size of a crow, is the smallest in the United States. It has put up with volleys of gunshot in the past, but somehow remains abundant and even rather tame. Because of its size and relatively sluggish flight, it is ignored by falconers.

Observation Guidelines
Along with the red-tailed hawk, the broadwing is the most common woodland hawk, and is a summer resident throughout the range. Some birds winter in Florida and Cuba, but most go all the way to Central and South America, avoiding the Gulf of Mexico by migrating via Texas. Using this circuitous route, they benefit from rising columns of deflected air (called thermals) which are lacking over water.

The broad-winged hawk is the only raptor that migrates in flocks. Each September they come pouring out of the North by the thousands, thrilling the ranks of bug-eyed hawkwatchers. If conditions are favorable, i.e., a cold front advancing on northerly winds, the hawks flow by checkpoints in groups of up to a hundred or more. Upon seeing a squadron of these hawks advance, novice birders tend to drop their binoculars, forget about keeping count, and simply stare in disbelief — as hawk after hawk cruises by out of nowhere, filling the northern sky with their buoyant, chunky bodies.

Paul Roberts, a former teacher and current editor, is anything but a novice hawkwatcher. He is the chairman of the Hawk Migration Association of North America, and once had the pleasure (and pain) of counting 10,213 hawks in nine hours. On September 13, 1978, while atop Mt. Wachusett in Princeton, Massachusetts, he and three others witnessed the largest broadwing movement recorded in the northeastern U.S. As Roberts remembers it, "I found a river of broadwings stretching from horizon to horizon. Some had already passed over us, gliding so high that we had initially failed to perceive them. We can't know how many birds had already passed from our view, but within the next fifteen minutes we tallied 2,387 broadwings, almost invisible to the naked eye, passing directly over the summit. Another 1,598 were recorded over the next half-hour. We were incredulous. Approximately 4,000 hawks in 45 minutes. Our necks and eyeballs ached, but with adrenalin surging through our systems, we were in a state of euphoric shock."

During the breeding season, the broadwing is found in most deciduous woods, and can be identified by the broad black and white tail bands, a rusty barred front, and white underwings. The tail is distinctive at great distances. In flight, the hawk's compactness and stubby tail distinguish it from larger buteos. When broad-winged hawks utilize warm bubbles of air to soar, they'll often spiral a mile high, coast along for several miles, and level off as the thermal cools. Then they tuck in their wings, close the tail, and rocket down in teardrop shape to another thermal, bound for tropical Peru.

Calls are exceedingly shrill, thin whistles, sounding like: Ta-weee. Broadwings are quite vocal, although many people mistake their calls for those of a smaller bird or even an insect.

BROAD-WINGED ON PREY   Photo by Henry B. Kane.

Natural History

Alert observers might spot a broadwing rising with a squirming snake clutched in its talons. The hawk then struggles, hovers for a few seconds, and ascends into a breeze that the snake no longer feels. Up and away the bird goes until it's out of sight, leaving the watcher as limp as the snake.

Besides having a taste for snakes, the broadwing also relishes toads, frogs, small birds, rodents, and insects. It is particularly fond of the caterpillars of big moths that are so common in summer. With extreme patience, it perches in a tree by the hour, watching for its next meal, and because of its omnivorous habits (even earthworms, fish, and crayfish are eaten), it rarely goes hungry for long.

Since this is the tamest hawk in the East — often moving only a few flaps away after being flushed — close encounters with humans are numerous. In 1840, John James Audubon told of a bird that was brought down by hand from its nest, then measured and drawn without apparent trepidation. J. Hooper Bowles reported in Bent's *Life Histories of North American Birds of Prey,* of another incident:

"The tail of the sitting bird could be plainly seen sticking over the edge of the nest, but no amount of pounding on the base of the tree would move her. Consequently, my brother climbed up, and much to our surprise she still remained on the nest when he reached it. I then climbed up and joined him, but the hawk stayed perfectly still and did not show the least sign of fear or anger. We stroked her and finally lifted her off the nest and tossed her into the air, when she flew to a tree not far away where she was soon joined by her mate."

When pairs arrive at their breeding grounds in April, they immediately start screaming at each other from separate perches. They also make small circles in the air and dart about playing tag. When they begin the chore of nest-building, it is usually 25 to 50 feet up in the main crotch of a hardwood.

At a slow pace, a stick at a time, they form the small nest, and then abandon it for a few days before laying time. It's loosely made of sticks and dead leaves, and lined with bark and greens — the greens often added daily, the old sprigs discarded with the beak. Birds will use the same tract of land for several years, but rarely the same nest.

After incubating for a month, two or three eggs hatch, off-white and blotched with brown. Hatching ordinarily occurs around late May near Washington, D.C., mid-June in New England, and late June in Michigan. The hawklets are attentively reared by both parents; they even cover the vulnerable nestlings with greenery if they're away for long. Within 30 to 40 days the young are fledged, with plenty of time remaining to prepare for migratory journeys of up to 4,000 miles.

Professor Robert Vernon, of Simmons College in Boston, told of a unique experience that Kimball Elkins had with nestlings in New Hampshire: "Years ago, he and his brother were out in the woods and found a broad-winged hawk's nest. The brother climbed the tree (20 or 30 feet up) to look in the nest. Before he looked in, however, one of the two downy young jumped out and fell ca-plop on the ground. Then the other one jumped out and it, too, fell. The birds were then banded. Since they needed both hands to climb the tree, they did not dare to put the young birds back in the nest, so they set them on a log beside the tree and left. (Nothing was seen of an adult all this time.) That night, after they got home, Kimball says they felt guilty about leaving the young out there, so the next morning they took a knapsack and went back, but the young were not to be seen. One of them climbed the tree, and behold, there were the young back in the nest! Kimball says there is no report of broadwings ever carrying their young."

When blueberries wane and loosestrife blooms in purple glory, and when swallows congregate on the wires, broadwinged hawks band together, young and old. They wait for the warm updrafts to lift them, or favorable winds to push them south. Then as a unit dozens of hawks abruptly forsake their native hardwood forests for the land of bananas and rubber trees.

YOUNG RED-SHOULDERED HAWKS   Photo © by Leonard Lee Rue III.

Chapter 7

RED-SHOULDERED HAWK

Buteo lineatus

Introductory Remarks

The red-shouldered hawk is a large buteo with narrow white bands on its black tail. It is infamous for its disappearing act during the past three decades. DDT and other pesticides have taken their toll on this species, but scientists are slow to concern themselves with the hawk's fate; compared with studies on the bald eagle and peregrine falcon, the redshoulder's plight has been ignored.

Ed Hanna, a 32-year-old Canadian, is one of the few who is interested in finding out its current status, and he has checked more than 300 woodlots near Toronto at his own expense. "I don't know how many proposals I've put in," he says, "mostly for small sums of money. The red-shouldered hawk hasn't got enough attention. There hasn't been enough noise for the public to become interested." If interest is not aroused soon, new birders may have trouble ticking it off their life lists.

Observation Guidelines

Although reportedly doing well in California, the red-shoulder is suffering in the East, particularly in northern sections where it competes with redtails for nesting sites. It is listed as "threatened" in New Hampshire, and is currently on the National Audubon Society's "Blue List" of declining species. It is an uncommon breeder throughout the East, and, where found, is a permanent resident from the latitude of Lake Erie south to Florida.

This buteo frequents the same type of habitat as the barred owl: wet and deciduous woodlands. Ed Hanna found that active nests are 42 feet, on the average, from water. The hawks generally prefer wooded floodplains and side slopes along ponds, swamps, or rivers. In Florida they are birds of palmetto hammocks.

Adults show banded tails, rusty underparts, and chestnut-red shoulders at close range. In flight, translucent areas, called windows by birders, are evident near the wingtips from below. Compared to the red-tailed hawk, the redshoulder has longer, narrower wings up to four feet long. It's also more active when it flies, flapping more and making tighter circles.

Calls are clearly-enunciated, descending cries of, Kee-yer or Kee-ah-yer, repeated often. It's the noisiest hawk in the woods and blue jays, themselves noisy, can imitate these calls almost perfectly, confusing even veteran birders. William Brewster wasn't fooled, though. Formerly of Cambridge, Massachusetts, and one of the most respected ornithologists in the last hundred years, Brewster wrote in his journal in 1892, "The blue jay's imitation is certainly good, but it never deceives me. It reproduces the form merely and lacks the essential quality of tone. This difference serves if the bird is near." Most other birders curse quietly to themselves after bushwhacking for a hawk and finding only a taunting jay.

Natural History

With its dingy coloration (less conspicuous than the redtail), the red-shoulder perches by the hour unnoticed. While perched, the dark eyes scan for any movement, and when it spots prey, the bird glides down on stiff wings and pounces. It soars only on a part-time basis.

Known foods include mice and other small mammals, birds, crayfish, grasshoppers, beetles, snakes, and especially frogs, since both prey and predator inhabit wetlands. Although called the hen hawk like the redtail, it's a misnomer, because the red-shouldered hawk takes very little poultry; there have been cases of hawks nesting within a half-mile of poultry farms without raiding. Around the barnyard they seem to prefer rats or carrion to delectable bantams.

Red-shouldered hawks are hesitant to attack humans, instead screaming and swooping overhead. In early spring, pairs court each other hundreds of feet in the air, wheeling, swooping, and calling all the while. Copulation takes less than a minute. Most pairs choose breeding territories in moist woods, and, more than other raptors, show a real affinity for a certain site — reusing it for years or even decades when offspring carry on the tradition.

Nests are built close to the trunks of large trees, often 35 to 50 feet above the ground. They take a month or more to make, less if an old barred owl or squirrel nest is used as a base. Nests are well built cups of sticks, lined with bark, leaves, down, and evergreen sprigs. White downy feathers on the ground beneath and fresh evergreens in the nest indicate that eggs have probably already been laid. The presence of shrieking parents removes all doubt.

On average, three dull white eggs, spotted with brown, are laid in early April, and both mates incubate, which takes about 28 days. As the young grow, they learn to squirt their excrement clear of the nest, leaving the nest clean but obvious raptor spoor in the form of white-wash far below. Within six weeks the young birds fledge, but the adults continue feeding them for some time.

Come October, hawks from northern latitudes drift southward as the leaves that once hid their nests tumble. By the first ice of the season, New England birds are gone and the only remaining traces are deserted nests that weather well — barren nests filled with fallen leaves and the hope of the hawks' return.

ROUGH-LEGGED HAWK   Photo courtesy of Cornell Laboratory of Ornithology.

Chapter 8

ROUGH-LEGGED HAWK

Buteo lagopus

Introductory Remarks

The aquiline rough-legged hawk is the only buteo in the East with a white rump and base-of-tail. Its scientific name is derived from the Latin, "buteo," meaning buzzard (Europeans still refer to buteos as buzzards), and from the Greek, "lagopus," meaning hare-footed. Because it breeds exclusively in Arctic regions, it has flown free of mankind and his environmental tampering. Only in wintertime, when birds move far south of their usual range seeking food, do they confront danger — guns in the hands of men who value lifeless trophies more than the lively free-soaring hunters.

Observation Guidelines

The roughleg breeds in healthy numbers all around Hudson Bay east to Labrador and Newfoundland, and also breeds in northern

Europe. People in the U.S. can expect to see occasional winter migrants from the Great Lakes to Maine, and south to Virginia. Anytime from October to April, observers searching open plains, agricultural areas, or coastal marshes might spot one of these big buteos propelling itself on stiff, wooden, yet powerful wings.

The species has two color phases: light and dark. The light phase is characterized by much white below, other than a black belly and two prominent wrist patches. Dark-phased birds have darker bodies and white only on the flight feathers. Both phases show a long white tail with a black band near the tip, and feathers cover the feet all the way to the toes, hence the name. This leg protection is probably an adaptation against the cold.

From afar, the roughleg can be identified by its bulky, dark frame, its impressive wingspan of more than four feet, and its habit of hovering on sluggish wings — a habit not practiced as much by red-tailed hawks.

Calls, uttered only at the nest, are penetrating, one-syllabled whistles that descend at the end. Birders hoping to hear this species must travel to Canada when mats of bear-berries reappear, their pale flowers replacing the white of receding snow.

Natural History

In its native Arctic, lemmings, meadow voles, and shrews form the basis of the roughleg's diet, but when the rodent supply dwindles with the approach of winter, the hawk has to go where the food is. Every three or four years the lemming population peaks and crashes dramatically, followed by a decline in the number of its predators. Foxes, not as mobile as birds, starve, while snowy owls and rough-legged hawks emigrate south, few to ever return.

Like an owl, the roughleg flies silently and hunts on dark days and at twilight, making it our most nocturnal hawk. It employs three methods of hunting: perching precariously on a slender branch while watching the ground; quartering low over meadows in the manner of a harrier; and hanging motionless on updrafts deflected by dunes or hills, the first six primary feathers spread like black fingers. A likely area to see a roughleg hunting in New England is the north shore of Massachusetts, especially at Salisbury Beach and Newburyport. To follow one of these hawks hovering in place over a tidal marsh and then sail for the sun setting over the dunes makes one appreciate winter.

Because of its languid flight, great size, and unsuspicious manner, roughlegs made easy targets during the fire-at-anything days. In 1925 William Brewster described the slaughtering of these hawks in western Massachusetts: "At Northampton lived two gunners fond of shooting hawks and very expert at it, who sometimes killed as many as twenty roughlegs in the course of a single day. The gunners commonly hunted them in an open buggy drawn by a well-trained horse over smooth, grassy, interval lands bordering on the Connecticut River, and shot at them mostly on wing as they flew from the tops of small, isolated trees, in which they were accustomed to perch. When approached in this manner, they seldom left the tree, until the horse was stopped within gunshot of it."

Where trees are present, the hawks nest in them, often as low as twenty feet, but on the open tundra a majority of birds use rocky ledges or the tops of cliffs. The shape of nests varies according to location; those placed on level rocks are nearly flat, while those on uneven surfaces are higher at the front and often lack a back. All of them are made of sticks, weeds, moss, and sometimes feathers. Nests used for several years become as large as an eagle's, and due to the cementing action of excrement, they're amazingly durable. Unoccupied nests can last a decade.

Like snowy owls, rough-legged hawks lay more eggs (up to six) in years when lemmings are abundant, but these plans can backfire if the lemming population crashes during the same season. The usual clutch size is three or four. Both parents incubate for about a month, and the babies hatch in late June or July. By the first week of September, immature birds rim the nest, huddled and ready to launch themselves into a new world of thermals, clouds, and snow. They scan the vast, forbidding tundra, fan their tails and take off one by one, no longer passive feeders but now active predators.

KESTREL (or sparrow-hawk)　　　　　Photo © by Leonard Lee Rue III.

Chapter 9

AMERICAN KESTREL

Falco sparverius

Introductory Remarks

Falcons are sleek birds of prey with pointed wings and narrow tails. The kestrel, formerly called sparrow hawk, is the only falcon with a reddish back, and is the smallest diurnal raptor in the East.

During the Middle Ages, when falconry was flourishing in England, a person's rank could be told by which species of falcon he or she toted around on the wrist. Royalty carried gyrfalcons, earls carried peregrine falcons, yeomen carried goshawks, and priests could fly the sparrow hawk. Today, with the population of the other three species greatly reduced, falconers are more apt to fly prairie falcons in the West and kestrels in the East, but even the streamlined kestrel couldn't outdistance the widespread ravages of toxic pesticides, especially in the southeastern U.S.

Observation Guidelines

The American kestrel is still relatively common, and throughout its range is a permanent resident. It is a raptor of open country, roadsides, and farmland, and is one of the few birds of prey that has adapted itself to civilization. Motorists can spot them hovering by the minute on manic wings over grassy highway borders.

The size of blue jays, male birds are rufous above with blue-gray wings and a black and white-tipped rufous tail. Females lack the gray wings, but both sexes have striking black and white face patterns with Fu Manchu-type "mustaches."

Kestrels and other falcons are easily differentiated from buteos by flight alone. Falcons are swift, erratic flyers, and only the kestrel habitually hovers. It also pumps the tail irregularly while sitting erect on a perch. During September, single birds leisurely vacate Canadian breeding grounds via the coast, gain momentum, and streak by the hawkwatchers' bleary eyes.

Nicknamed killy hawk, the kestrel emits a rapid series of Killy, Killy, Killy! These sharp calls, given year-round, have a flicker-like staccato quality, and indicate that a bird has encountered an intruder. They are calls of aggression.

Natural History

Diets vary according to season and locality. In the summer, kestrels eat mostly grasshoppers and crickets, but towards winter they switch over to mice and small birds. They also hang around bird feeders, waiting for juncoes, titmice, house sparrows, or any other easy meal.

For eight years, Donald Heintzelman studied kestrels in Pennsylvania and learned that they are also fond of cicadas. In 1962 there was an outbreak of these woodland insects, and the birds left their familiar farmland and entered the forest edge to hunt. Of the kestrels studied that year, cicadas accounted for 17 per cent of their diets. Wildlife species rarely leave habitats that they're suited for because it makes survival all the more difficult. Kestrels are adapted to open country (hovering in deep woods is hard to do), but in this case they tried it probably because the bulky insects were easy prey.

A bird on the hunt routinely perches atop telephone poles, wires, or dead trees, watching the ground. Then, quick as a mousetrap spring, it swoops down, striking and ensnaring the prey with its talons. If the prey is a rodent or bird, it tears off the top of the head with its hooked, notched beak. At other times it hunts by hovering, body tilted up facing the wind on beating wings. In either case, food is lugged back in its claws to a favorite station and ripped apart. There's barely enough left over to feed an ant.

If there's such a thing as a playful raptor, this is it; there are many published accounts of individual kestrels toying with several larger hawks. Songbirds seem not to fear them, however, and kestrel attacks on people are rare.

They make engaging pets, as Olive Rhines learned during her 25 years with the Hartford Audubon Society. "One kestrel in particular was a delight," she remembers. "Brought to me before it could fly, but in fine physical condition, still wearing fluffs of down, it quickly adapted to my foster care. It would reach eagerly for bits of hamburg or liver while perched on my glove hand, and when not feeding was content to stay in a screened room in the barn. By implanting parts of small trees in the dirt floor, I created a fairly natural environment for my charges.

"The kestrel learned to come to my wrist at my whistle, and as soon as I felt confident in his attachment to me, I took him into the yard for schooling. This consisted of showing him live grasshoppers and earthworms in the grass, and it was not long before he learned to pounce and devour the bait. By the time he had graduated to live field mice, I knew he was ready to fly on his own, an exercise he had been practicing with brief sallies from one perch to another. His experiments in flying soon took him into the trees from which he would return to me for a reward of food. His forays became lengthier until the day when I felt he was able to shift for himself, and so, with some trepidation, I left him out one night instead of securing him in the barn loft.

"I need not have worried; he was awaiting breakfast early the next morning. The taste of freedom went well, for he stayed away more and more until he finally disappeared for good, but not without one last farewell. One day while out in my yard, I saw the kestrel flying at some distance. With perfect aim he 'stooped,' landing in a matter of seconds on my bare head. A hearty meal of meaty tidbits and he was off again, never to return."

Nonbreeding territories of a hundred acres or more are used for hunting, and are defended during the fall and winter. Breeding territories, twice that size, are used for mating, nesting, and feeding, which the kestrels defend from March to June. The male, who arrives at the breeding ground before the female, rises and dives near the nesting site, calling at the top of each plunge. Copulation takes place on a branch perhaps a dozen times a day for up to six weeks. After paired for the season, the female ceases her hunting, lingers near the nest, and from then on the male feeds her until the young hatch.

Males usually choose the nesting site, which is often a natural cavity 15 to 30 feet up in an old tree overlooking a field or orchard. Abandoned squirrel or woodpecker holes are also utilized, as well as man-made nesting boxes. The kestrel is the only native hawk that will nest in a birdhouse. Persons wanting to attract this species should place a raw wood box on a tree in the open, facing east or south. Put sawdust on the floor (kestrels add no lining themselves), even though they might push it aside, and cut a hole three inches in diameter in the front. The handsome falcons will eventually move in.

Three to five eggs are laid on alternate days late in May around New England, and in April down South. Females do most of the incubating, the males doing about four hours daily. During this month-long period, females grow so attached to the eggs that they can be lifted off the clutch by hand, although this is not recommended because desertion is always a possibility.

The young hatch within a few days of each other and immediately the male has to feed them and his mate while she broods. When she stops her daytime brooding, she then helps her mate with feeding for the rest of the nestling phase. The hawklets stay put for a whole month but the nest does not become extremely soiled because they shoot their feces up on the walls where they dry.

Massachusetts birder Paul Roberts, who had kestrels nest in his house eaves just outside Boston, watched one of the birds fledge. "I saw a young kestrel," he wrote the author, "perched on the edge of the roof, just above the gutter. Somehow, the bird had climbed out of the gutter, and it was obviously uncertain as to how to return to the safety of that natal gutter. Ever so slowly, the little falcon inched its way up the steeply sloping shingles, stopping every 6-12 inches to look back down almost wistfully. But it apparently seemed safer to keep climbing up rather than challenge the force of gravity and risk

Kestrel House

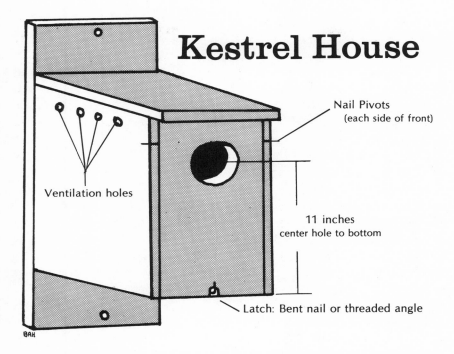

Nail Pivots (each side of front)

Ventilation holes

11 inches center hole to bottom

Latch: Bent nail or threaded angle

Face house southwest in field or on field edge; at least 10 feet up.

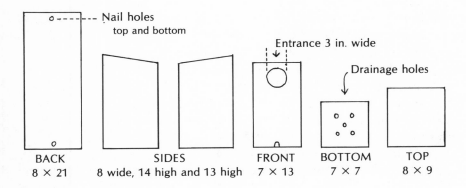

Nail holes top and bottom

Entrance 3 in. wide

Drainage holes

BACK
8 × 21

SIDES
8 wide, 14 high and 13 high

FRONT
7 × 13

BOTTOM
7 × 7

TOP
8 × 9

KESTREL

Photo by Henry B. Kane.

falling to earth. The bird finally reached the top of the roof, and then edged its way forward, along the top, until it came to the very tip of the roof.

"I wondered what would happen next and how long it would take to happen. (I had been watching this show for some time.) Suddenly, a blur out of nowhere dove at the nervous kestrel, barely missing the young bird. I questioned what this mysterious attacker was, when suddenly it struck again. An adult kestrel buzzed the roof at great speed, literally knocking the young hawk from the roof with its talons. The hawklet fell from the roof, flapping its wings furiously. Slowly it achieved altitude, and with great effort was able to make it across the street, where it plopped down on the lowest point of the roof of a friend's house. Ever so slowly, the exhausted little bird crawled up the roof until it sat on the very pinnacle and could survey the route it had just flown. Obviously, the parent kestrel had intended to force the fledgling to fly — and it had."

Once fledged, juveniles practice their flying close to home, returning nightly to the nest hole with the mother. After two weeks of this, the young hunt for themselves, sometimes in combined groups of ten or more if food is plentiful. Meanwhile, the adults are undergoing a molt, preening almost continuously. As autumn nears and easy prey diminishes, each bird is on its own. Family ties are severed forever. Only by chance would siblings find themselves both defending the same territory next spring.

MERLIN (or pigeon-hawk)   Photo © by Leonard Lee Rue III.

Chapter 10

MERLIN

Falco columbarius

Introductory Remarks

Formerly called pigeon hawk, the merlin's scientific name originates from the Latin, "falco" for falcon, and "columbarius," a noun meaning pigeon keeper. It is the only small falcon in our range with a heavily banded tail.

Merlins have never been falconers' favorites because of their habit of "carrying," that is, after killing prey they take off with it instead of standing over the body, waiting for the falconer.

Mercury levels in urban Canadian birds declined in the 1970s, but organochloride levels did not. Nonetheless, merlin populations on the whole are stable if not increasing, because, as Richard Fyfe of the Canadian Wildlife Service discovered, they are much more resistant to DDT and DDE than either peregrine or prairie falcons. When DDE residues of 15 to 20 parts per million (ppm) are present in peregrine eggs, reproductive failure is assured, while the critical threshold for merlins is about 30 ppm.

Observation Guidelines

The merlin breeds mainly in Canada, with northern Maine supporting a few nesting birds each year. It is still threatened in parts of its range, and is overall a sparse migrant in the East, wintering mostly south of Delaware. William Clark, director of the National Wildlife Federation's Raptor Information Center in Cape May, New Jersey found that most merlins pass by between September 15 and October 7. Approximately 80 per cent are immatures. Cape May flights peak between 2 and 3 p.m., and it is a real possibility that merlins migrate nocturnally, since birds seen hunting at dusk are gone by the first light of day. Northbound spring birds over Cape May peak from April 20 to May 10.

An inhabitant of coniferous forests while breeding, the merlin also visits marshes and open country out of season. Look for a grackle-sized falcon with a dark appearance, the male showing a blue-gray back, the female's a dusky brown, and both sexes showing buffy, brown-streaked breasts. While migrating they fly in a direct line at treetop level.

Calls are rapid, excited cheepings not as piercing as those of the kestrel. It is usually silent except at the nest.

Natural History

The merlin is a bird killer, regularly feeding on starlings, woodpeckers, doves, jays, sparrows, warblers, etc., and is the only raptor in the range capable of catching swallows on the wing. It can take birds up to the size of a pigeon, and will attack flocks of birds, especially shore-birds on migration. Thomas McIlwraith wrote in 1894 of a merlin dashing into a band of blackbirds in Ontario: "How closely they huddled together, as if seeking mutual protection, but he went right through the flock and came out on the other side with one in each fist."

The feisty merlin perches on an exposed pole, post, or tree, and when it spots a bird or dragonfly, chases until the prey escapes in a thicket or is caught and picked apart. Merlins are so pugnacious that they'll even pursue other larger hawks or gulls — sometimes to the falcon's undoing.

Fearlessness is one of the merlin's major traits, and it extends towards humans, too, although birds demonstrate restraint when ornithologists are checking nests. Copulation is often performed in more than one territory, and males will display for a week or so and then abruptly leave the area.

Nests are placed high in heavy timber, cliffs, or on old birds' nests. Dr. Harrison Lewis wrote of a Labrador nest in an unusual location. "It was on the ground, among the reindeer lichen on the summit of a small knoll. A black spruce tree which had grown here for many years had died, leaving a confused snarl of stiff dead limbs. The pigeon hawks had placed their nest beneath this shelter. The nest, which was about six inches across and one inch deep, was a depression in the soil, here composed of sand and rotten wood, and was lined with a few small scales of bark, picked by one or both of the hawks from the trunk of the sheltering tree. Four eggs rested on these bits of bark. One hawk flew from the nest when I approached it, and they both scolded me vigorously, charging repeatedly to within a few feet of me, as long as I remained in the vicinity."

Four or five whitish eggs speckled with brown dots are laid in late May and on through June, depending on location. The female starts the month-long incubation as soon as the first egg is laid, thus the young hatch at intervals. In lean times the larger chicks are fed first, and the younger ones can starve to death. This action, possibly looked upon as cruel, is actually advantageous to the species because it allows at least *some* healthy offspring to survive.

Due to the merlin's penchant for the Far North, and the difficulty of locating nests, its current breeding status is uncertain. One place it is studied, albeit fleetingly, is at Lighthouse Point near New Haven, Connecticut, one of the best hawkwatching spots on the East Coast. Only since the early 1970s have organized watches been held there, but unlike other New England lookout stations, merlins seem to favor the Point. At least they're counted more regularly there.

Many of them pass over the water out of sight of land, so only at places like Lighthouse Point are they counted at all. Well over a hundred are now seen there each fall by avid birders standing sentinel beside their spotting scopes. When one flies overhead, rowing in the air pigeon-fashion, the people admire the dark, flapping missile and shout with arms raised like fans watching a home run ball arching over the centerfield fence. And like those baseball fans in chilly autumn, the birders are instantly warmed, elated, then drained, hoping for one more head-turning image to last them during the off-season.

PEREGRINE FALCON   Photo by William S. Clark.

Chapter 11

PEREGRINE FALCON

Falco peregrinus

Introductory Remarks

This news-making raptor, formerly called duck hawk, is the only large falcon with prominent black sideburn markings.

During the Middle Ages the peregrine falcon was one of the few "noble" hawks — hawks that attack from above, called stooping. It was favored because of its grace, mild temperament, and awesome speed; it can fly 60 miles an hour on the level, and has been accurately clocked plunging at 82 mph. (Reported speeds of up to 180 are exaggerated.)

This favorite of nobility was rudely decimated in the late 1940s because it could no longer reproduce itself. Eggshells had become weakened by continued spraying of DDT, which peregrines ingested through the bodies of smaller prey birds. Eggs cracked or were eaten by deranged parents, and few remained intact long enough to develop. Finland's estimated population of a thousand pairs before World War II dwindled to 20 pairs by 1975. Similar catastrophes occurred elsewhere in Europe and North America. Worldwide populations shrank.

The American peregrine was declared an endangered species in 1970 by the U.S. Fish and Wildlife Service, and was subsequently given protection under the Endangered Species Act of 1973 — the first law in the country to recognize the importance of preserving habitats. Enter Dr. Thomas Cade. In 1970, as director of the new Peregrine Fund at Cornell University's Laboratory of Ornithology, he set goals of hand-raising captive birds and returning them to the wild. Shortly after initiating the program he said in an interview, "We should see peregrines nesting again in the eastern United States. We hope by the end of this decade."

The most difficult aspect of hand-raising peregrines was how to get the eggs fertilized. Captured females readily lay, but males are reluctant to copulate in the new surroundings, so artificial insemination was employed along with mate-switching. In 1973 the project succeeded in rearing 20 nestlings from three fertile pairs. Working in his spacious, unheated barn in Ithaca, New York, Dr. Cade and his staff increased the breeding stock, and a year later they began to release some of the young birds. Two were put on the roof of a ten-story building in New Paltz, New York and two were planted in a wild peregrine's nest in Colorado.

The New York pair, appropriately named Adam and Eve, were fitted with tiny radio transmitters by Heinz Meng, who is a falconer, biologist, and co-worker of Dr. Cade's. Three months after release, both birds were believed dead because food put out on the roof went untouched. In addition, the New York State Conservation Department had received an anonymous phone call telling them to "get those killer birds off the campus." Shortly thereafter the shredded wing of an immature female was found near the New Paltz campus.

The Colorado pair fared better; wild foster parents raised the adopted young, who later also took to the wild. In 1975, on an island at the Aberdeen Proving Grounds near Chesapeake Bay, Maryland, Cade put four nestlings in a man-made eyrie. There, 70 feet up on the tower, all four fledged successfully, and one of them, nicknamed Scarlett, has since resided on a 33rd-floor building ledge in Baltimore. She raised five foster chicks in 1981, and Fish and Wildlife officials hope that she finds a beau and becomes a natural breeder. Also in 1981, Cornell University reported that 84 hand-raised peregrines were released, making a total of 353 since 1974.

Dr. Cade saw his prediction of naturally-nesting falcons by 1980 come true in the spring of that year, when two pairs mated, incubated, and raised their own young near Barnegat Bay, New Jersey — probably the first wild peregrines to fledge young east of the Mississippi since the 1950s.

In early June, 1981, New Hampshire also made headlines widely read by concerned birders, conservationists, and ecologists: While rock climbing with a companion, mountaineer John Bouchard was strafed by two peregrines. On June 8, U.S. Fish and Wildlife official Rene Bollengier and Tom Sears, a volunteer from Cornell's Peregrine Fund, located the eyrie, which proved to be an ancestral one not used previously for at least a quarter-century. Two young falcons were raised. This successful nesting in the White Mountains was the Northeast's first since 1953, and became the only instance of peregrines nesting on a natural crag in the eastern United States. (The last known active site was on Mount Tom, Massachusetts, where falcons had nested continuously for almost a hundred years.) The National Guard Bureau in Washington, D.C., recently assured skeptical ornithologists that low-level, high-speed fighter jets that train over the White Mountains will avoid the celebrated nesting area.

Observation Guidelines

The peregrine falcon is an endangered species on national and state levels, breeding in the wild in these states only: New Hampshire, Maine, New York, New Jersey, Delaware, Maryland, Pennsylvania, Virginia, North Carolina, and the District of Columbia. The outlook is grim, but it's better than it was in 1975 when an extensive survey of old nesting sites found not a single breeding bird east of the Rocky Mountains.

Formerly the species bred across North America, wintering from Massachusetts south to Central and South America, although it was never numerous. Today, other than scattered birds from captive stock, the peregrine breeds sparingly in the Arctic. People wanting a glimpse of the speedy one should head for the East Coast in October to keep watch.

Birds can be identified first as large falcons, then as peregrines when they draw closer, revealing bold face patterns. The flight is a combination of short, quick wingbeats and brief glides. Birds often ignore updrafts — heading through instead of riding them — and fly much higher than merlins.

Calls, not likely to be heard, are actually rapid, raspy cackles. The falcons also emit assorted wails at the eyrie.

Natural History

Like its miniature cousin the merlin, the peregrine is a bird killer. In a hunting range of over a hundred miles, it slays ducks, gulls, pheasants, and songbirds by the score. On migration, shorebirds are a specialty, and in cities, pigeons. Joseph Hagar, former Massachusetts State Ornithologist, described a pigeon's undoing: "In the instant before the strike, the falcon had arrived at a point perhaps 12 feet behind the pigeon and a foot below it, when she suddenly changed her direction, extending her talons, shot up across the pigeon's back, and at the moment of passing, grappled her prey, apparently by the body just behind the wings, so that the two birds swept on as one, without the least perceptible pause. One instant the pigeon was flying desperately; the very next it hung a limp bundle, with drooping wings and neck, in the talons of its terrible pursuer."

Peregrines normally attack from above or the side, but occasionally from below. They attack over water whenever possible because the prey has no cover. Depending upon prey size, they either grab hold with the talons, or knock the kill out of the air and descend to pluck and eat. Their nostrils have a system of baffles to deflect the rush of air; the falcons could not otherwise breath during their rocketing stoops.

The peregrine is known as a marauding prankster because when its appetite is sated, it sometimes speeds through a flock of harried birds without striking, scattering the flock in all directions. Physical contact with humans at nesting sites is rare.

They indulge in long courtship displays in March, the male spiralling up and then plunging, alternately rolling, circling, and calling on the descent. He also feeds the female, who is more likely to remain closer to home once they are mated.

Historically the peregrine nested on cliffs overlooking water, but tall building ledges have replaced them in the industrialized 20th century. Between 1941 and 1951, employees on the 20th floor of the Sun Life Assurance Company building in Montreal took their coffee breaks gawking at hawks. During those years, 42 eggs were laid, but only 21 hatched. One young falcon pounced on a pigeon but its momentum carried the hawklet against a rooftop where it broke its neck. Such are the hazards for raptors growing up in the big city.

Peregrines don't make an actual nest, even on cliffs. The female merely scrapes out a hollow an inch or two deep and a foot across. She typically lays four eggs in April, and does most of the incubation, which lasts 33 to 35 days. Individuals have been known to live 15 years or more.

The peregrine falcon breeds and migrates around the world, but it was extirpated in the United States. As its natural environment continues to be altered and invaded by mankind, it will be ironic if surviving 21st-century birds reproduce solely on rooftops above man-made canyons.

MISSISSIPPI KITE   Photo by Allan D. Cruickshank.

Chapter 12

MISSISSIPPI KITE

Ictinia mississippiensis

Introductory Remarks

Kites are shy, relatively obscure raptors of southern climates. All four species recorded in the United States are graceful flyers, and all except the endangered snail kite of Florida's everglades have pointed wings like falcons. The Mississippi or blue kite is the only falconlike bird with an all-black tail.

Unfortunately, its numbers too have decreased through the years. South American wintering grounds are crucial for continued survival. Tropical hardwood forests still cover about 40 per cent of the continent, but the human population is skyrocketing as industry begins to rival agriculture. The lumber industry is just getting off the ground; cabinet wood like ebony and mahogany, found along wide jungle streams, will be much in demand, and since this is where the kites dwell, something will have to give. If the birds cannot winter safely, they cannot return to reproduce.

Observation Guidelines

In the East, this species breeds locally from Arkansas and Louisiana across to the Carolinas, and is expanding its range northward, especially along the Mississippi River. A reliable (and intriguing) place to find kites in Florida is just south of Tallahassee, bordering the Wakulla River. Guided boat tours cruise the water, flanked by cypresses and river birches — all draped with Spanish moss, lending an aura of veiled mystery. The haunted, repeated wails of limpkins and the ethereal flight of kites make such excursions unforgettable.

Individual birds stray as far as the Great Lakes and New England. Since about 1975, more of these vagrants have been sighted in springtime at Cape Cod and in southern New Jersey. There is even speculation that kites are now nesting in Salem or Cumberland Counties, New Jersey, along the Delaware River. By late September most birds have left their secluded breeding grounds and migrated to Central and South America.

Blue kites live in tall timber, mixed scrubland near water, and semi-open country. They can be found in pine woods or in mixed groves of cottonwood, sweetgum, and oak.

Pigeon-sized but more slender, the kites have blue-gray backs, black wingtips and tails, and pearly heads. Their breasts are pale gray and eyes shine deep orange-red. When viewed from above in flight, whitish patches show at the rear of the wings, but since such occasions rarely present themselves to observers, the black, unbarred tail suffices for positive identification.

"Its flight," wrote John James Audubon in 1840, "is graceful, vigorous, protracted, and often extended to a great height. At times it floats in the air as if motionless, or sails in broad, regular circles, when, suddenly closing its wings, it slides along to some distance and renews its curves."

Calls, although seldom heard, are series of two or three clear whistles, reminiscent of an osprey. Only at the nest are birders likely to hear them.

Natural History

Mississippi kites are tireless flyers, spending the daylight hours snatching up cicadas, grasshoppers, and dragonflies out of the air, and pouncing on occasional snakes, lizards, and frogs. "When in pursuit of a large insect or a small reptile,'' Audubon continued, ''it turns its body sidewise, throws out its legs, expands its talons, and generally seizes its prey in an instant. It feeds while on the wing, apparently with as much ease and comfort as when alighted on the branch of a tall tree.'' They have marvelous eyesight; birds have been seen accurately stooping for locusts from a hundred yards up.

Kites build compact stick nests at treetop level — up to about 120 feet high — and line them with green leaves or Spanish moss. The height at which they place their nests, and the surrounding foliage, makes the structures extremely difficult to find. Nests tend to be used for several consecutive years.

The females lay one or two off-white eggs in May, which hatch a month later. By August immature birds are heavily streaked and have barred tails, quite unlike their parents. By the time that pickerelweeds have sent up their three-foot blue spires along sluggish streams, kites of all ages are gathering in loose flocks before they set sights for Paraguay.

SWALLOW-TAILED KITE

Photo by William A. Paff.

Chapter 13

SWALLOW-TAILED KITE

Elanoides forficatus

Introductory Remarks

This extra-large version of the familiar barn swallow is the only raptor with a forked tail.

When Robert Ridgway was growing up in rural Illinois during the late 1800s, he used to stare at swallow-tailed kites reeling gracefully over the prairie. By the summer of 1910, while employed as an ornithologist with the Smithsonian Institution, he saw two of the last individuals of the species that would be recorded in Illinois for some time. Fifty years later, their range, which formerly included much of the eastern United States, had been reduced strictly to the South.

For unknown reasons the species has gradually disappeared from this country, favoring more tropical climes. Even its stronghold, Florida, is no longer as accommodating as it once was. Drought conditions in the Kissimmee Valley of South Florida have plagued this region for years, caused by land development and the drainage of wetlands. Water used to flow from the Kissimmee River south to Lake Okeechobee, and spilling into the everglades, but now there isn't enough flowage to evaporate and transpirate, resulting in less water falling from the atmosphere as rain. The hydrologic cycle has been disrupted.

During Florida's normal rainy season (June-September), droughts are disastrous for wildlife and humans alike. In 1982, Nathaniel Reed, former Assistant Secretary of the Interior, said that Everglades National Park is "...on the brink of death." Populations of wading birds such as herons, egrets, and ibises have declined as much as 90 per cent since 1940, according to park personnel. Kites are following in their wake.

Observation Guidelines

The swallow-tailed kite currently breeds in Louisiana, Mississippi, Alabama, Georgia, Florida, and South Carolina. (It formerly bred as far north as Wisconsin.) Florida still boasts the healthiest numbers; in central and southern parts of the state between March and November, kites are fairly common. Most birds spend the winter in South America, while some remain in southern Florida.

Irregular vagrants to the Northeast have been increasing since 1975, but the significance is questionable since most sightings are made near Cape May, New Jersey and Cape Cod, Massachusetts where birders abound. Additionally, the number of birders in the field greatly increased during the 1970s, and these strays now seen with mounting regularity could have been previously overlooked.

Swallowtails inhabit river bottoms, marshes, and particularly cypress swamps. Bald cypress swamps are eerie, shadowy wetlands dominated by moss-draped trees rising out of still waters, where sullen alligators loll about. Kites and other birds add fleeting dashes of life to an otherwise dreary scene.

The swallow-tailed kite has a black back and tail, and a white head, breast, and underwings. It is the size of an osprey, but has shorter, pointed wings. The deeply forked tail is diagnostic, and the bird flies as fluidly and as swiftly as any. Only peregrines and swifts are faster flyers.

Calls are high, shrill peeps and whistles. When several birds fly together, they twitter like chimney swifts, but overall they're silent.

Natural History

Swallowtails often hunt in small groups, flying back and forth over familiar territory. They look for locusts, bees, beetles, snakes, and frogs, seizing the prey with their talons, and eating on the run. Robert Ridgway wrote of their feeding technique in 1905: "It went over the ground as carefully as a well-trained pointer, every now and then stopping to pick up a grasshopper, the feet and bill seeming to touch the insect simultaneously. They were very fond of wasp grubs, and would carry a nest to a high perch, hold it in one claw, and sit there picking out the grubs."

Paired birds indulge in spectacular aerial rituals — rising, falling, and madly swooping after each other by the hour. After mating, they build a nest together, using their talons to collect sticks, needles, and Spanish moss. One observer in Minnesota found more than 200 separate pieces of lichens in a nest, which had been carried individually from a marsh a mile away. Nests in Florida are usually situated in tall slash pines at the edge of cypress swamps.

The laying season extends from mid-April through May, the two or three eggs hatching in about three weeks. Both parents defend the young from all intruders, and even attack people foolish enough to climb over a hundred feet high just to inspect the nestlings.

Swallow-tailed kites are best seen, however, from a distance, when they fan their pointed wings and tails, cutting the air like boomerangs. Seeing one of them skim over the water and dip down for a bath and a drink makes a person realize the ecological value of swamps.

NORTHERN HARRIER   Photo by Kenneth W. Gardiner.

Chapter 14

NORTHERN HARRIER

Circus cyaneus

Introductory Remarks

Formerly called the marsh hawk, the harrier gets its name from its harrying tendencies. (To harry is to plunder, ravage.) Harriers are a family of hawks with slim wings and tails, and our northern species is the only member in North America. Its white rump is diagnostic.

During the 1960s and 1970s, wildlife biologist Frances Hamerstrom of the University of Wisconsin studied populations in a 40,000-acre area in Portage County, Wisconsin. She discovered irregular fluctuations in yearly nesting successes, and because DDT was applied to the study area during the mid-1960s, she suspected that this was the cause. After DDT was banned in Wisconsin, harrier productivity increased and is currently stable.

Observation Guidelines

Since it is a habitat-sensitive species and its prime habitats — freshwater marshes — are disappearing, the harrier is a local breeder, and is even considered threatened in some New England states. In the East it breeds sporadically from Canada to Illinois and east to Pennsylvania and the Maryland coast. Records at Hawk Mountain Sanctuary in Pennsylvania show that immature birds make up the late summer flights, October brings immatures and females, and in November the males straggle by. The migration season, from late August through November, is the longest of all raptors. Birds winter from coastal Massachusetts to Florida, Cuba, and beyond.

The discerning harrier is found only in fresh and saltwater marshes, open grasslands, and sloughs. Males are pale gray above and white below; females are streaked brown. Both sexes have white rumps, long narrow wings and long narrow tails. When airborne, the wings are often outstretched above the horizontal plane, vulture-like. They are ponderously slow, erratic flyers who seem to dislike strong winds. The overall appearance of a harrier hunting is akin to a gull buoyantly tilting and tossing, head down, over windy surf.

It is usually a silent bird, but near the nest lets out high, nasal whistles and some lower-pitched, squirrelly chirps. The male's voice is deeper than the female's.

Natural History

Unlike most other hawks, the harrier flies close to the ground when hunting (about 20 feet up), flapping and gliding back and forth trying to rustle up some meat. At this low altitude, it is able to see *and* hear the prey, and its sense of hearing is excellent. The hawk's disk-shaped, owlish face is thought to aid in amplifying sounds in the manner of a parabolic reflector. When a rodent is detected, the hawk stops and flutters or hovers above, then drops and feasts on the spot.

Harriers rarely perch on trees, preferring low stumps, fence posts, or the ground. After tacking around all day on its winter range, covering possibly several square miles, birds retire to expansive, overgrown fields to roost. They do so communally, often on a hilltop in groups of 30 or more. Each ground roost is a matted-down impression that's whitewashed with droppings, and rimmed with pellets from repeated usage.

NORTHERN HARRIER   Photo by Kenneth W. Gardiner.

For years harriers were thought to be destructive to young ducks and gamebirds, but in 1931 Herbert Stoddard proved otherwise. Out of 1,100 harrier pellets that he found at a Georgia roost, only four contained quail remains, while 925 contained the remains of cotton rats, which eat quail eggs. Unfortunately, several of the hawks there had already been killed by Bureau of Biological Survey employees who figured they were doing farmers a favor. Because cotton rats are also injurious to farm crops, the plan of shooting their natural predators (harriers) doubly backfired.

Besides rats, harriers pick up field mice, shrews, birds, frogs, and young rabbits. Any living creature within their home range is fair game. They even settle for carrion.

A few years ago, Paul Roberts had an opportunity to compare the harrier's flight with the short-eared owl's. "Suddenly, upwind from the owl," he wrote, "an adult female marsh hawk appeared, hunting low over the marsh and tidal stream beds. The owl moved swiftly, quickly reaching and rising above this new intruder. The harrier is one of the most beautiful and graceful hawks in flight. Today, how-

ever, I learned that the marsh hawk is slow and cumbersome compared to the short-eared. The owl flew at one o'clock above the inter-
loper. The marsh hawk acted oblivious to the mouser above it, until
suddenly the owl nose-dived at the hawk. The harrier shifted in mid-
air as though to avoid a collision, but it continued to work its way
into the wind. The owl swiftly wheeled above the harrier and buzzed
it once again, reminding me of the old World War II films in which a
quick, maneuverable American fighter would harass the larger, but
much slower and more vulnerable enemy bomber. The marsh hawk
maintained both its decorum and its steady pace, seemingly wanting
to escape the owl's anger as quickly as possible but without appearing
to do so out of fear.''

Harriers prove tough defenders of their territories, however,
especially when young birds are in the nest. They frequently attack
human trespassers, as A.D. DuBois realized, writing in Bent's *Life
Histories* series: ''While I stood near a nest, trying to arrange a tri-
pod and camera, the parent marsh hawk repeatedly struck me on the
head. In one of these onslaughts she lifted my hat and dropped it on
the ground. Her claws penetrated the hat sufficiently to scratch the
scalp.''

Also stunning, but more peaceful, are the flight displays by males
over March breeding grounds. These spring rites please potential
mates as well as gazing birders. The male rises a few hundred feet in
the air and divebombs the female within ten feet of the ground, then
sweeps up, somersaults and heads down again. He repeats these giant
aerial U's 20 or 30 times in a row. Occasionally the female rises to
meet him on one of his descents, but normally she's hunting or
nodding approval from her perch.

Both mates help build the ground nest, using their bills for carrying
grass and small sticks, and their feet for larger sticks. Nests can be
flimsy or well-made depending on location; higher, more substantial
homes are built in wetter areas such as tidal marshes, where there is
flooding potential. Outside diameters average two feet, inside
diameters eight or nine inches.

Birds lay five or six (but up to nine) bluish white eggs in May
around the Northeast, and in late April toward Florida. While the
female is incubating, the male will fly in with food for her, and call.
She rises, flips on her back, and with her talons catches the food

dropped by the male from 15 to 20 feet above...a unique and elaborate reception.

Hawklets fledge in approximately a month, then spend the rest of August learning how to hunt before wandering south ahead of the adults. As the studies by Frances Hamerstrom indicate, most birds won't return to the same breeding grounds the next year. Instead, they'll be patrolling over the cattails in another marsh with another mate.

BALD EAGLE

Photo © by Leonard Lee Rue III.

Chapter 15

BALD EAGLE

Haliaeetus leucocephalus

Introductory Remarks

Our national symbol, the bald, or American, eagle is the only large brown bird with a white head and tail.

Back in 1782, when the Continental Congress designated the bald eagle our national bird, the species probably nested in every state of the Union. Today, because of rough treatment by man, anyone desiring a sure sighting must travel to Alaska, where an estimated population of 30,000 birds still exists.

An expanding human population, accompanied by a loss of habitat, shooting, and especially the use of chlorinated hydrocarbon residues (DDT, etc.) have been the culprits. By World War II eagles were rapidly disappearing, regardless of the 1940 Bald Eagle Act. This act protected eagles in the Lower 48 but excluded Alaska until 1953 when protection was provided by an amendment. At that time, the National Audubon Society reported that about a thousand pairs existed in the Lower 48, a figure that stands today. It is estimated that this figure is only one per cent of the original population. Ironically, some eagles depend on the vacillating hand of man; wintering birds in Sullivan County, New York rely on hydroelectric power generation to create open water for their fishing.

In Maine, a state that had the dubious distinction of recording the lowest reproductive success of any 1973 eagle population in North America, help was needed in a hurry to ease the eagle's plight. The help came from Minnesota. In May, 1974, U.S. Fish and Wildlife officials took three eggs from nests in the Chippewa National Forest, Minnesota, and put them in nests along the lower Kennebec River in Maine. The world's first bald eagle egg transplant was a partial success: two hatched, but one of the two chicks died shortly thereafter.

From 1974 to 1981, the number of active nests in Maine rose steadily from 34 to 64, and in 1981 49 eagles were raised — the most in twenty years. Maine's eagle comeback is due to several factors: DDT ceased to be used in 1970; devoted people have helped, such as wildlife biologist Frank Gramlich and about 2,000 citizens who watch over the eagles for him; and the University of Maine's Bald Eagle Project and a lot of public education have made people more aware. This comeback can be reversed by gunners, however. At least eight bald eagles were killed in Maine in 1981, according to Dr. Ray Owen, professor of wildlife resources at the University of Maine. "We're really wild over this," he said. "It's undoing everything we've been trying to do." The Bald Eagle Protection Act (BEPA) allows only Indians to keep eagle parts for traditional ceremonies.

"Laws are enforced," says Louis Locke, wildlife biologist from Madison, Wisconsin. "We had a young man in Platteville, Wisconsin who paid a $1,000 fine for shooting an immature bald eagle." In that same year, 1980, Patience, a radio transmitter-equipped eagle that was trapped in Glacier National Park, Montana, was tracked by Harriet Allen for three months before she lost the beep signals near Ontario, Oregon. She picked up the signals again by airplane, and landed to find Patience's body under a foot of rubbish in a dump. The landowner confessed to the shooting and paid a $2,500 fine, half of which went to the National Audubon Society raptor project that Allen was working on. The maximum fine is $5,000, which might

YOUNG EAGLE   Photo courtesy of Maine Department of Inland Fisheries and Wildlife.

seem severe, but if the species becomes extinct, we'd have no one to blame but ourselves, and there would be little solace in looking at stuffed specimens, dollar bills, mail boxes, or presidential seals.

Observation Guidelines

The bird is currently an endangered species in parts of its range, particularly the South. It has been extirpated from much of this country, but Alaskan and Canadian populations are healthy. In the East, eagles still regularly breed in upstate New York, Maine, Michigan, and along the Carolina and Florida coastlines. Despite pollution, the Chesapeake Bay area supported 95 known nests in 1981, the best results there since the early 1960s. Two of the nests had gray squirrels nesting practically side by side with the eagles.

Eagles spend up to five months on their wintering grounds, which are scattered throughout the range. Quabbin Reservoir in Massachusetts, for example, supports up to a dozen eagles. There they fish in Boston's water supply and, when it's frozen over, feed on deer that break their legs and die on the ice. Persons with wanderlust or cabin fever should go to McDonald Creek in Glacier National Park, where several hundred birds winter, decorating the western hemlocks like ornaments. Any ice-free river, lake, or pond also has potential. Starting in September, migrating birds can be seen almost anywhere, especially over mountains on days with a northwest wind. Adults are seen more often than young birds.

At 10 to 12 lbs., the bald eagle is the largest eastern raptor, and is identified by its white head and tail, and its massive yellow beak and feet. Immatures are dark all over except some white on the underwing linings. Eagles, soaring on wide, flat, stiff wings spanning up to seven feet, cannot be mistaken for hawks.

Calls are gull-like cackles or whines, somewhat timid-sounding for such imposing birds of prey.

Natural History

Eagles feed largely on dead and dying fish. It's not that they can't catch live fish, they're just lazy opportunists. They also eat other carrion, and live waterfowl, rabbits, and squirrels. Although rarely observed, they have a notorious reputation for robbing ospreys of their catch in mid-air.

They hunt either by swooping low, trying to startle the prey, or by soaring high, using their phenomenal eyesight. (Eagles are reputed to detect sizeable carcasses two miles away.) They also hunt cooperatively, as Ronald Joseph, raptor biologist with the U.S. Fish and Wildlife Service, observed in Fairfield, Utah in 1977. He saw a pair sweeping over the sagebrush, one a few yards above the other. The female landed and ran after a pheasant, and when the pheasant rose, the male seized it.

Bald eagles tolerate crows and ravens who often feed simultaneously on the same carcass, but they don't tolerate golden eagles who usually displace the more mild-tempered bald. When humans approach an active nest, the adults scatter. Attacks are very rare.

Nests are eyries built near the tops of tall, live trees or cliffs. The same eyries are used for years, and are made of sticks up to two inches in diameter, and lined with moss, grass, pine needles, or, on one occasion, a tablecloth. After several years, nests can become huge, eventually toppling under their own weight. It is common for a nest to be three feet high and five feet across; one, the so-called Great Nest of Vermilion, Ohio was a landmark for 35 years. When measured in 1922, three years before it blew down, it stood 12 feet high, 8½ feet across, and was believed to weigh over a ton. A mighty eagle perched on that nest was dwarfed like a child on a house.

After an incubation period of 35 days, the female hatches one or two relatively small white eggs around December in Florida, and April or May towards the Northeast. Both parents dutifully care for the young until they're ready to fly, which they learn on their own. When the right day dawns, the parents cease bringing food in; instead, they offer it at a distance, starving the young into the air. After the young fledge, the family stays together the rest of the summer and disbands in favor of more deeply-felt northerly winds. It takes fully three years for eagles to mature, and they can live for half a century.

Only man's unrelenting shooting, and the destruction of suitable habitats (particularly wilderness areas) threaten eagles in the Eighties. Watching one of these birds — big even at a distance — soaring strong overhead in regal majesty, is a heartening experience. One can only admire and wish it well as it drops behind lonely highlands.

GOLDEN EAGLE

Photo by Neal Clark.

Chapter 16

GOLDEN EAGLE

Aquila chrysaetos

Introductory Remarks
This is the only eagle that is all dark below. The generic name, aquila, is taken from the Latin meaning eagle. ("Aquiline" today means curved like an eagle's beak.)

The golden eagle was highly revered by the American Indians, who called it Thunderbird, messenger of the Great Spirit. White men, typically, have done little but persecute it. Between 1943 and 1963, upwards of 20,000 were picked off by hired assassins in airplane shootoffs, mostly in Oklahoma and Texas. A belated amendment to the Bald Eagle Protection Act was passed in 1962 to include the golden eagle in order to protect both species in cases of mistaken identity. The effects were minimal. Although shootoffs are now banned, the shameful practice still occurs.

Several hundred golden eagles are electrocuted each year on power lines when their wings touch two or more lines simultaneously. Some power companies in the West are doing something about it: they erect perches above the wires; they install larger insulators; and they space the wires farther apart or else raise the middle ones.

Irrigation has also taken a toll. Irrigated farmland, where small rodents abound (of little use to the eagles), is displacing arid grasslands, where rabbits, marmots, and ground squirrels live, which are prime eagle fare. Energy project development in the West might be another obstacle for the eagles to dodge in the near future.

Observation Guidelines

There are approximately 35,000 golden eagles in the United States today, the majority found west of Texas. Canada has a healthy population, and a few pairs breed in the Adirondacks and down in the Appalachians as far as the Great Smoky Mountains National Park. Historically, it's always been an uncommon species in the East.

Some birds reside year-round on their breeding grounds, but many of the northern ones, pushed by November's northwest winds, winter in the northeastern and central states, and can be found in any type of habitat. Basically, however, it is a bird of deciduous foothills and mountainous forests.

Adults are dark with a gold patch behind the head and neck; immatures in flight flash white underneath at the base of the primary feathers, and also at the base of the tail, thereby distinguishing them from immature bald eagles. Golden eagle tails appear longer than the bald's. Aquila is among the fastest flyers, diving in excess of 60 miles an hour.

They are mainly silent, reserved birds, but occasionally they scream out high-pitched, gull-like notes that are amazingly weak for such a big bird.

Natural History

Golden eagles can kill deer, antelope, calves, lambs, raccoons, and woodchucks, but are more likely to chase rabbits, hares, and ground squirrels. Some waterfowl and game birds are also taken, along with rattlesnakes, but the snakes sometimes strike first, killing the feathered attackers. Seton Gordon wrote an account in Bent's *Life Histories* series about how strong an eagle can be defensively: "The eagle was devouring the carcass of a blue hare when a fox sprang from the surrounding heather and seized the great bird by the wing. The eagle made an attempt to overpower its antagonist by striking with its wings, but that would not compel the aggressor to quit its hold. At last the eagle succeeded in raising the fox from the ground, and for a few minutes Reynard was suspended by his own jaws between heaven and earth. The eagle made a straight ascent and rose to a considerable height. After struggling for a time, Reynard was obliged to quit his grasp, and descended much quicker than he had gone up. He was dashed to the earth, where he lay struggling in the agonies of death. The eagle made his escape, but appeared weak from exhaustion and loss of blood.''

Golden eagles hunt from either a lofty perch, where they constantly bob their heads in jerky movements, thus aiding their range-finding, or soar high. Their dives are fast and accurate, and they can spot a mouse at 400 feet.

Golden eagles have some of the largest defended breeding territories of all birds — up to 40 square miles. Eyries are generally located in a commanding position on a rocky cliff or in towering oaks, sycamores, or pines. They are large and bulky, made of branches, roots, and plant stems, and lined with hay, green grass, leaves, or bark.

Eagles reaching four or five years old can breed, with two or three eggs usually laid. The attractive white eggs, which are lightly blotched or speckled with shades of cinnamon, were highly prized by egg collectors who risked their lives scrambling up rock walls and tall trees, attempting to secure another species.

The female does the incubating, but the male assists by feeding his mate on the nest, and later brings food to her; she then feeds the eaglets. The more dominant nestling (in most cases the larger female) sometimes turns on the smaller sibling and pecks it to death or forces it out of the nest. Known as the "Cain and Abel conflict," this behavior results in one strong eagle being raised instead of two possibly weak ones.

Eaglets fledge in about ten weeks with assistance from the parents. There are eyewitness accounts of adults pushing a fledgling out of the eyrie, allowing it to fall for a hundred feet or so, then swooping down and catching it on their back — no subtle warning, but an effective one.

Never a prolific breeder in the East, the wary golden eagle will probably endure in wild, isolated regions of our mountainous parklands. There, perched atop ancestral crags, remnant populations will be safe as long as eagles and parks are protected.

BLACK VULTURE   Photo © by Leonard Lee Rue III.

Chapter 17

BLACK VULTURE

Coragyps atratus

Introductory Remarks

Vultures, or buzzards as they're known in the American West, are the black sheep of the raptor family. Bare-headed scavengers, they feed on carrion and refuse. As depicted in many western movies, they connote nothing but death and dying in the land of the purple sage, but in reality they serve a vital role as nature's sanitation squad, thus checking disease. Three species, including the rare California condor, inhabit North America. All possess excellent eyesight and are magnificent gliders; they can survey the ground from a thousand feet and soar up to six thousand.

The black vulture is the only big, all-black bird with white patches near the wingtips. It seems to have the unusual ability to learn new tricks about flight, as bird-bander Edward McIlhenny discovered in 1935. He saw a vulture over Louisiana that was tailgating a mail plane. The airplane was doing about 150 miles an hour, and the bird kept pace 200 feet behind. By staying slightly above the slipstream, it benefitted from the upswelling air, saving energy and getting through with the mail.

Black vultures have few enemies. Even humans have restrained from shooting them except when they gather in large flocks near young farm animals. Vultures are much more revolting to look at (up close) than feared as predators.

Observation Guidelines

The black vulture is a permanent resident from Virginia to the Gulf of Mexico. It is a common breeder and is expanding its range northward. In the Northeast it's an irregular vagrant usually seen in the spring.

Compared to the more inland turkey vulture, the black is a beachcomber, and also hunkers close to towns and cities, especially near garbage dumps and slaughter houses.

Black vultures can be differentiated from turkey vultures by their shorter, square tails, much shorter wingspan, and by flight behavior. They flap faster and more often than turkey vultures, and do a lot of brief, labored gliding. Because of their relatively short wings, they appear heavier in the air.

Other than grunting, hissing, or blowing, black vultures are silent. "Adults and young, when cornered or annoyed," wrote Edward Thomas, "give a rasping, hissing snarl, also described as a snore, and half-way between a wheeze and a squeal. The young give this frequently in the presence of the parents. In addition, I heard the adult give a low, croaking 'Coo,' very much like a one-syllabled coo of the domestic pigeon."

Natural History

This ancient-looking bird feeds mainly on carrion, but also preys on live lambs, piglets, herons, and cormorants. Animal excrement is not passed up, either. Ornithologist Alexander Wilson described a feeding flock near Charleston, South Carolina in 1832: "I counted at one time 237, but I believe there were more, besides several in the air over my head and at a distance. I ventured cautiously within thirty

BLACK VULTURE FEEDING   Photo © by Leonard Lee Rue III.

yards of the horse carcass, where three or four dogs and twenty or thirty vultures were busy tearing and devouring. On observing that they did not heed me, I stole so close that my feet were within one yard of the horse's legs, and again sat down. They all slid aloof a few feet; but seeing me quiet, they resumed as before. Some of them, having their whole legs and head covered with blood, presented a most savage aspect.''

These gorgers have weak feet and hobble about with difficulty, but in the air, though not as graceful as the turkey vulture, they're in their element. Their sense of smell, used for locating food, has been debated since 1835, when Audubon and John Bachman conducted experiments on both species. To summarize: decomposed carcasses which were hidden for 25 days went undetected, and a blinded black vulture didn't notice carrion within inches of its nostrils. Audubon flatly concluded that both species locate food by sight, not smell. Similar experiments have since been tried, but it wasn't until the 1960s that black vultures were shown *not* to have a great sense of smell, but that the turkey vulture does — and uses it. Audubon was half right.

Black vultures are gregarious, often perching and roosting communally. Audubon and Bachman visited a huge roost in a Charleston, South Carolina, swamp and wrote, "When nearly under the trees on which the birds were roosted, we found the ground destitute of vegetation, and covered with ordure and feathers, mixed with the broken branches of the trees. The stench was horrible. The trees were completely covered with birds, from the trunk to the very tips of the branches." The men estimated birds in the thousands.

While perched, especially in wet weather, vultures move little. They appear listless. When the sun shines, they habitually spread out their wings to dry. Although fairly approachable, a person would be wise not to get under them while perched, because if disturbed, the birds regurgitate foul-smelling matter in unison. No form of acid rain is pleasant.

Avian courtships are always hard to watch because they usually don't last long. You have to be at the right place at the right time and know what to look for. In his 1840 classic, *Birds of America,* Audubon told of this species' performance: "At the commencement of the love season, which is about the beginning of February, the gesticulations and parade of the males are extremely ludicrous. They first strut in the manner of the turkey cock, then open their wings, and, as they approach the female, lower their head, its wrinkled skin becoming loosened so as to entirely cover the bill, and emit a puffing sound, which is by no means musical."

The bird makes no true nest; eggs are laid on bare earth or at the bottom of stumps or inside hollow logs. It favors saw palmetto, sawgrass, or yucca thickets, and even slinks into caves when trees are scarce. For some reason it decorates the area around the eggs with bright objects (probably collected at the dump) such as pieces of plastic, glass, bottle caps, cigarettes, etc.

In early spring the female lays a couple of spotted eggs, and has her mate assist in incubation, which lasts about a month. They feed the young by regurgitation; nestlings insert their beaks down their parents' throats and ingest milky substances using a nibbling action. At two months old they fledge, rise on tropical thermals, and instantly transform from homely underlings to handsome sky gliders.

TURKEY VULTURE   Photo by Kenneth W. Gardiner.

Chapter 18

TURKEY VULTURE

Cathartes aura

Introductory Remarks

This is the only black raptor that flies on wings held in a shallow V, or dihedral. Like other vultures, the turkey vulture has a bare, ugly head which allows it to poke inside carcasses without attracting too many parasites that would otherwise cling to feathers. The name of the American vulture family, Cathartidae, is from the Greek, meaning cleanser, which refers to the birds' habit of picking bodies to the bone.

Because vultures do a service for man by cleaning up roadsides and farmlands of fetid carcasses, and because the birds themselves stink, they've been left alone. Few are killed or studied at close range. A person has to have a weak nose and a strong stomach to approach their rank nesting sites, especially those found in caves.

In the early 1900s the turkey vulture bred only as far as New Jersey, but by the 1950s it had reached Massachusetts and was rapidly extending its range northward. Possible factors to account for this spread are: moderation of climate; an increase in deer population, hence, more carcasses; and the construction of new highways, resulting in more roadkills. Whatever the reasons, the expansion has been relatively swift. It used to be that people travelling from the Northeast could look up and sense the South around Virginia, but today the South hangs everywhere in the air — symbolized by ubiquitous buzzards.

Observation Guidelines

Turkey vultures currently breed all over the East, from Lake Ontario to central New England and south to Florida. Birds arrive on northern breeding grounds in March and stay until September. Most birds winter south of Ohio.

These are raptors of the air, commonly seen lilting over open land, highways, and woods. At close range they show a red, turkey-like head and exceedingly large nostrils. In flight, they are identified by their two-toned black wings that span six feet, and by the way their wings are angled slightly upwards. They often tilt and tip from side to side, rocking to the beat of unheard breezes. Turkey vultures are some of the most efficient, well-balanced creatures of the air, as they have to be since carrion is not always available. They seldom flap.

Vultures are usually silent. Only when feeding in a group or if disturbed at the nest will birds let out high hisses and snarls that befit their nasty looks.

Natural History

The vulture's main dish is soft, ripe carrion. A bird flops down on the ground, waddles up to a decaying body, and aims for the eyeballs. Then it rips off the skin and eats the muscle and everything else. Nothing remains except bones. After gorging itself, the vulture struggles to take off, leaning forward and loping like Groucho Marx until it finally labors up and away.

Recent tests have proven that turkey vultures (but not black vultures) can detect food by smell if the carrion is smelly enough. Simulated gases of decomposition have even attracted them when no meat was in sight. Aside from smelling or seeing the food itself, they

TURKEY VULTURE   Photo by Kenneth W. Gardiner.

might also be aided by insects. Carrion beetles, which locate dead matter within minutes, possibly lure vultures, as reported in Bent's *Life Histories* series: "In November, 1926, some dead fish were put out near Harvard House [in Cuba] to attract beetles, but were stolen by turkey buzzards the first day. The bait had been hidden under fairly large stones. They may, indeed, have smelled the fish, but it seems just as likely that they saw the insects which collected and which would have given the set away to any intelligent human being. Near Santa Marta, Columbia, in 1928, the same sort of thing happened, for when dead iguanas were put out they were invariably discovered by vultures, even when the baiting was done in scrubby woods. The most rational explanation in this case seemed to be that the birds had heard the carrion-drawn flies."

Shortly before sunset on winter evenings, they drop down from the sky to roost communally in tall, dead trees. There they ruffle up, preen, and settle to sleep. Not until an hour or so after sunrise do they stir; ground fog has to clear first, and sun-affected thermals take time to develop, thereby enabling them to soar for hours with hardly a flap.

Most nests are on the ground, in stumps, or on remote cliffs, but Andrew Pickens reported to Arthur Cleveland Bent a nest in an old barn in Anderson County, South Carolina. "I found the eggs," Pickens wrote, "two in number, on the refuse of the stable floor, close up in a corner. About ten feet away a domestic hen was brooding on her nest in a pile of forage, the two being separated, however, by a low partition. The vulture could gain access to its nest through a small window in the stable, or through a door at some greater distance."

Nests are well-concealed because the rancid carrion smell attracts predators, especially when adults are feeding the young. Two blotched eggs are laid on wood chips, sawdust, or gravel anytime from March in Florida to May in New York. Both sexes incubate, and when the eggs hatch a month later, the downy chicks are fed by regurgitation. The nestlings' eyes open immediately and the babies move about, hissing, within a week. After eating, sunning, and stretching their wings for another two months, the young ones fledge, but sometimes the parents continue to feed them until migration occurs.

In September and on through October, mountaintop birders can identify vultures a mile away. These enormous black birds with upturned wings are unmistakable. They're also enviable. Thirty ebony bodies dipping and playing in the wind make one yearn to join them and find out what it's like to be a mile high. Maybe they only see vague shades of death, but an hour spent with them would last a person a lifetime.

Chapter 19

AUTUMNAL PROCESSION: A HAWKWATCHING PRIMER

"When you see the high-flying hawks," said Paul Roberts, "there's something about the majesty on wings that is hard to describe. In bunches they look like giant moving mobiles. There's a certain dedication to hawkwatchers that not all birders have. Hawkwatchers *have* to be patient. I go and gamble. I derive satisfaction from knowing the birds are there, even if they're at the limits of my vision."

Roberts is one of the more serious amateur birders in New England and is chairman of the Hawk Migration Association of North America, whose aims are: "To advance the knowledge of bird of prey migration across the continent; to provide a bank of data on migration for the use of ornithologists; to help establish rational baselines for future monitoring of bird-of-prey populations; and to measure and understand the behavior of birds of prey better than we do, the better to defend their future right to living room and survival on the planet."

The Association, whose membership has doubled in the past three years, collects data sheets and other observers' reports that are sent to regional editors, who then write up seasonal reports in a lengthy newsletter. The standardized field records are keypunched into computers at the Migratory Bird and Habitat Research Laboratory in Laurel, Maryland then forwarded to Hawk Mountain Sanctuary in Pennsylvania, where they are stored for future use.

Each fall, qualified leaders conduct hawk watches and complete their daily report forms, including such hourly information: maximum visibility, temperature, sky appearance, wind speed and direction, flight altitude and direction, and the number of each raptor species. Today, about 12,000 birders make annual pilgrimages to Hawk Mountain, while others try hilltops, dunes, airports, or even rooftops. As Paul Roberts says, "Anyone interested in hawks should always keep one eye skyward during the months of September and October. Migrating hawks can be seen anywhere, in any weather, at any time of day. A few years ago, a birder decided to spend the day repairing the roof of his house. While on the roof, he saw more than 4,000 broad-winged hawks, and good numbers of several other species pass over his home." (Birders are notorious for dropping everything when the birds go by.)

Several years ago, Paul Roberts was initiated into this habit-forming pastime. "It was a glorious September day on Mount Tom," he recalls, "the most famous hawkwatching site in New England. The observation tower was crowded with hawkwatchers enjoying the magnificent spectacle of hundreds of broad-winged and other hawks migrating south. Suddenly, in the early afternoon, the activity increased. Small but frequent kettles of broadwings could be seen moving along the horizon. With all this activity, someone suddenly shouted for us to look up. Directly overhead, seemingly less than fifty feet above the tower, were hundreds of broadwings, hanging almost motionless in the air. They were so close we had to drop our binoculars to see them well. Hawks and humans were eyeball to eyeball, each observing the other. The hawks craned their necks left and right and then moved on. No one on the tower uttered a word. Spontaneously, everyone burst into a joyous applause. We saw some 2,400 hawks that day, and I became a hawkwatcher."

Birding in general and hawkwatching in particular have grown in popularity during the past decade, and, according to Roberts, "We're still uncovering new watch sites, and people are just beginning to understand how complex hawk migration really is." Besides Hawk Mountain, other known hot spots include: Little Round Top, New Hampshire; Mount Wachusett, Massachusetts; Bald Peak and Lighthouse Point, Connecticut; Cape May Point, New Jersey, where an estimated 200,000 raptors file by each fall, making it the best place for hawkwatching in North America; Hook Mountain, New York; Assateague Island, Maryland; and Hawk Ridge, near Duluth, Minnesota.

At Hawk Ridge Nature Reserve overlooking Lake Superior, a hawk comes into view every half-minute on the average, from late August to early December. In 1975, over 65,000 raptors were recorded by Molly Kohlbry — almost three times the number recorded at the more famous Hawk Mountain. There are now 150 regularly manned stations, mostly in the East, and more and more people are spending their weekends counting birds of prey. With more experienced counters, the total number of raptors recorded over the years has risen, yet data can be deceiving; a few years ago, Kohlbry tallied more than a thousand sharp-shinned hawks on one weekend, making it appear that sharpshins are faring well, which they aren't. Kohlbry and other astute observers put little value in such counts. They participate mainly for the camaraderie and the thrill of seeing so many raptors in a short period of time. Even one sighting can be memorable. Kimball Elkins, a veteran field man from New Hampshire, at Mount Tom once saw a peregrine falcon rob an osprey of its catch. The fish had only fallen about 20 feet when the falcon snatched it up and took off.

Migratory birds move south in the fall as decreasing daylight affects their biological sensors. They migrate by day or night, somehow recognizing and following outstanding land features. Mountains, valleys, rivers, and lakes serve as signposts during the day, while celestial bodies seem to guide them at night. Most hawks migrate diurnally, using ridges for guidance and for the assistance of currents created by solar heating of valleys. They glide as much as possible, utilizing these currents for maximum conservation of energy. After all, some hawks, like the peregrine, go from Alaska to Argentina, a trip of 5,000 miles. How the birds make these long hauls and wind up on the very same wintering grounds year after year remains a mystery.

Hawks and other birds seem intuitively to predict developing weather patterns, so watchers can look at these patterns and improve their chances of witnessing big flights. Generally, if a low pressure system has just passed, and a cold front advances on northerly winds — especially north-westerly — raptors should soon be moving. Broad-winged hawks, however, frequently move through with little wind, instead riding bubbles of heated air, called thermals. Large flights even occur in fog or rain, although observers are seldom around to record them.

One never knows when prime time will come; Paul Roberts was once stationed atop Mount Wachusett in Massachusetts, and saw hardly a hawk between 8 a.m. and 4 p.m. He learned later that an hour after his departure 500-plus broadwings were seen. It's a personal challenge to endure eight or ten hours scanning the skies for the big birds that, due to distance, often appear rather small. Sightings are very sporadic. It's feast or famine, and watchers often starve. But when the hawks cruise by in the fall, they're sometimes in bulging concentrations called kettles, so that in one day watchers can see more hawks than most people do in a lifetime.

September belongs mostly to the broad-winged hawks, which account for more than 50 per cent of all raptors annually recorded. On the 17th, in 1981, the author felt that this was the Big Day. Conditions had not been favorable for several days, and besides, the 17th is often the magical date. The hawks had to be accumulating somewhere, waiting to launch themselves south, so on this 70-degree, partly cloudy morning, the stage was set on a local New Hampshire hilltop. A gentle northeast wind flipped red maple leaves over in flashes of crimson. A hundred or more blackbirds flew in a ragged flock towards the lake far below. A chipmunk filled its cheeks with beechnuts and scurried along a stone wall. Restlessness reigned.

After a buteo appeared out of the Northeast, coming right overhead, it was followed by others in a long and increasingly widening column. They poured by, 30, 40, 50 silently-rowing broadwings, filling the northern sky. I muttered an expletive and marveled at the age-old parade. I stopped counting, staring with awed, earthbound eyes. After passing over the hill, they bunched together, swarming higher and higher on an invisible thermal. Then one hawk broke away from the frenzy, and bulleted down on tucked wings. The rest followed suit, searching for another thermal to carry them to Connecticut for the night.

Several minutes later, another kettle formed out of nowhere. This one was larger, containing about 80 hawks. During the next hour I ogled kettles of 40, 100, 35, and 60. I was delirious. Just before leaving, a lone bird beat leisurely above, impressive even at a half-mile. I had hoped for a grand finale, but when an adult bald eale soared directly overhead, my hands trembled around the binoculars. I wasn't prepared for such a stimulating visit — even on a self-fulfilled Big Day.

Fall migration means warblers to some people, maybe geese, shorebirds, or even monarch butterflies to others, but to a growing number of hardcore birders, early autumn connotes hawks and only hawks. They withstand the sore necks, the waiting, the cold. They keep looking up, for that's where they seek inspiration. Their reward is viewing the hawk hordes that come pouring out of the blue North on September's boreal winds.

SCREECH OWL TAKING OFF AND IN FLIGHT   Photos © by Leonard Lee Rue III.

Chapter 20

OWLS THROUGH THE AGES

Since earliest recorded history, owls have frightened, mystified, and intrigued mankind. With their fixed, forward-facing eyes staring from big heads that can swivel 300 degrees, they make interesting, yet unsettling, images that long endure. These stoic masters of the night are the only birds in the world that can blink the upper eyelids, and they hoot or wail loudly and fly without a sound. Who isn't enchanted by such bizarre birds?

Owls are extremely well-equipped to hunt at night. They collect any available light with their large corneas (larger than ours), which allow more light to enter the lens of the eyeball. Their eyes are roughly the size of ours, and they can see at night about as well as we can during the day, with three-dimensional vision. Specialized ear openings hidden behind their light-colored facial disks detect high rodent squeals. And primary flight feathers are softly fringed in velvet, permitting silent approaches.

The word "owl" is from an Indo-European root, "ul," meaning to howl, and through the centuries man has been baffled by owls of all kinds howling in the dead of night. The Greeks associated owls with their goddess of wisdom, Athena, who was portrayed with an owl's head. The Romans, however, changed the owl's image, representing it as a bird of ill-omen. The death of Augustus was supposedly predicted by the hooting of an owl (owls can see into the future), and it is said that before Emperor Commodus Aurelius died, an owl came by and sat in his room. Even the scholar Pliny reported the superstitions that death follows the owl which perches on a house, and that a calamity happens whenever one roosts in a public building.

For such a wise, solitary bird, it has meant nothing but trouble for people; in *Macbeth,* "It was the owl that shrieked, the fatal bellman which gives the sternest goodnight." And, "Lizard's leg, and howlet's wing, for a charm of powerful trouble, like a hell-broth boil and bubble."

Many American Indian tribes viewed owls as both good and bad omens. Maine's Penobscot Indians, for example, believed that a screech owl, if mocked, would burn up the mocker in his camp, but they also regarded the barred owl as a camp guardian who warned of approaching danger. To the Hopi Indians, horned owls brought summer heat for their crops, and in the tales of the Pueblo Indians of New Mexico, burrowing owls were "priests of the prairie dogs".

To counteract evil omens, charms were developed around the world, undoubtedly with mixed results. Turning pockets inside out, or tying a knot in a handkerchief, or throwing salt on a fire all supposedly stopped a screech owl from hooting. A broom laid across a door stopped owls from bothering people at night.

Times and attitudes change through the years. Now, plenty of people would love to be bothered by owls, to see and hear these elusive birds. They are valuable predators who help maintain balance and diversity by feeding on the most abundant nocturnal prey. Perhaps their predatory habits are what infatuate Robert Schell of Marlton, New Jersey. He and his wife campaigned in 1980 to have the owl replace the eagle as America's national symbol. They created Patriotic W. (Wisdom) Owl, a six-foot-tall costume with American flags on each wing. The head is shaped like the Liberty Bell, and he dons the thing at any patriotic event. Owls have flown a long way for a long time to attain such status today. They are not "good" or "evil" creatures. They are simply unruffled birds of prey that come around the cabin once in a while and leave us in the dark.

SCREECH OWL

Photo by Henry B. Kane.

Chapter 21

SCREECH OWL

Otus asio

Introductory Remarks

The screech owl, the only small owl in the East with ear tufts, does not screech. The barn owl screeches.

Although people still fear this harmless gnome, it doesn't fear people. It's the most suburban owl of the lot, even nesting in birdboxes, and there's a certain owl that's been residing in a Rockport, Massachusetts, cemetery for over six years, sunning itself on a low branch to the delight of local birders. A Duxbury, Massachusetts family found one perched on their Christmas tree in their home on January 15, 1981. They were removing ornaments from the Scotch pine when Ruth Switzer's mouth dropped. "I didn't say anything for a minute," she said. "Then I told the kids there was an owl in the tree, and they didn't believe me. My first reaction was that it was frozen, but it was very much alive." The bird had apparently hidden itself while the tree was in the barn for two weeks before Christmas. Although the owl underwent a serious weight loss, it's a wonder that it survived at all — undetected — for a month in a busy household.

Observation Guidelines

The screech owl is a common permanent resident all over the East as far north as central New England. It is essentially non-migratory, but some birds disperse southward in winter. It regularly haunts cemeteries, old orchards, suburban parks, and open deciduous woods, but because it is active only after dark, it's often overlooked.

There are two color phases: rusty-red and gray. This dichromatism varies with geography, and is not based on age, sex, or season. There are simply red birds and gray birds, even within the same family. Gray birds roosting close to tree trunks in daylight look just like dead stubs — with ear tufts flared and yellow eyes closed.

These robin-sized owls have two distinctive calls. The primary one is a mournful, descending whinny, similar to a horse, which is uttered anytime after dark and often throughout the night. The other call is a rapid series of hollow, vibrating notes that carry well in the open. Both are spooky.

Natural History

Screech owls eat practically anything: large moths and beetles, caterpillars, cutworms, snails, frogs, bats, and small rodents and birds, to name a few. Bold hunters, they sometimes attack prey bigger than themselves and even turn cannibalistic. There is an account from Mendham, New Jersey of an apparently starving owl that came down a chimney and pulled a canary from its cage.

Elliott and Kathleen Allison, respected birders for over 30 years, witnessed a possible first in January, 1956. They heard an animal crying outside their Dublin, New Hampshire home and followed the critter with a flashlight. It turned out to be a screech owl, and when they approached closer, it retreated, dropping a little saw-whet owl on the snow. The prey was nearly the size of the predator.

When not out hunting, or being hunted themselves by great horned owls, the screech owl retires to a tree cavity or low perch. If approached in the open, it goes into a hiding pose, stretching up and freezing, relying on its cryptic coloration. If the ploy fails, the "dead stub" suddenly transforms into a squat owl — eyes wide open and bill clicking like castanets.

Olive Rhines, from Hancock, New Hampshire watched assorted behaviors while working for the Hartford Audubon Society. "The most amusing and endearing of my raptorial orphans," she wrote to the author, "were the screech owls, of which there seemed to be an endless supply. One in particular became a special pet, delighting the family and our friends with its antic behavior. Instead of relegating it to the barn, 'Pookie' was given the run of the house and quickly chose certain spots as favorite roosts, which simplified the necessity of placing newspapers strategically under each perch. He chose to spend the nights in one of the bookcases among the bird books, and for meals would show up at a clothes rack in the laundry. His chief form of locomotion was his two feet. He would lurch along, bowing and nodding in the most amusing way. It was always startling to a visitor to observe this strange bunch of feathers marching silently into the room, glaring with piercing eyes in all directions. He was a real ham and seemed to enjoy his practice flights, when he would often land unannounced on my shoulder and gently tweak my ear with his bill.

"We hated to let him go, but there came the day when he had been fully taught in the ways of retrieving live prey and in strong flying tactics. We finally released him, after which he remained close by for a few days. Like the rest of my bird charges, he eventually disappeared for good, and, I hope, for a long life in the wild where he belonged."

Screech owls raise families in natural tree cavities, abandoned nesting holes of flickers and pileated woodpeckers, and in building crevices. They also use birdboxes with entrances of at least three inches in diameter. Because they usually nest below 30 feet, nosy birders can easily peek in. Incubating birds do not budge, as Thoreau found out in May, 1855: "After a while," he wrote in his journal, "I put in one hand and stroked it repeatedly, whereupon it reclined its head a little lower and closed its eyes entirely."

In April, four to six pure white eggs are laid on leaves, wood chips, or other debris. By July the young owls have scattered into the blackness of the night. They'll be seen again some day, getting soundly berated by mobbing songbirds. They'll turn away, stuffy and defiant. Then, when they've had enough, they'll flee for shelter in the forest gloom.

SHORT-EARED OWL

Photo by Kenneth W. Gardiner.

Chapter 22

SHORT-EARED OWL

Asio flammeus

Introductory Remarks

This day-flying owl is identified by its streaked, tawny breast and its irregular, moth-like flight. The generic name, asio, was a Roman word for a horned owl; the specific name, flammeus, is Latin for flaming, which, albeit an exaggeration, refers to the brown coloration.

Because the species is active part of the day, and inhabits marshes, duck hunters have shot many of these owls over the years. The draining of wetlands has taken an even greater toll, and this habitat loss has forced the National Audubon Society to include the short-eared owl on its Blue List of declining species.

At Vancouver International Airport during the 1960s, owls and hawks were a nuisance to aircraft. Between 1963-1967, more than 500 raptors (chiefly short-eared owls) were trapped and removed, and attempts were made to keep the grass bordering runways short, so that rodents would not abound and attract predators.

Observation Guidelines

Shortears breed throughout Canada, around the Great Lakes region, and very locally in the Northeast, but their summer status is not well known. They winter irregularly from Massachusetts to Florida any time from October to April, and during this season can be seen along coastal beaches, marshes, dunes, or gathered at dumps where they search for rats.

Dr. Arthur Borror, professor of zoology at the University of New Hampshire came upon an odd sight one January day in 1973. "I was taken to a roosting site," he wrote the author, "of a group of about two dozen short-eared owls in a family cemetery in the Finger Lakes region of central New York. Our entry into the cemetery put many of them to flight. They'd been spending the days huddled, one behind each tombstone! Each tombstone bore mute evidence of their occupancy — a few pellets. Later dissections showed the pellets to be composed almost exclusively of meadow vole remains."

These long-winged brown owls look as though they've been in a boxing match; black areas circle the eyes, accentuating the yellow pupils. Their one-inch ear tufts rarely show. In flight, large buffy wing patches show from above, and black wrist patches from below. Like the marsh hawk, they fly low and occasionally hover, but their flight is more erratic, more bounding than the harrier.

Calls, seldom heard except at the nest, sound like they're coming from a fox pup instead of an owl. The birds merely bark and yip. Shortears, largely silent, are no exception to the rule that open-country owls are less vocal than owls of the deep woods.

Natural History

As Dr. Borror's account indicates, the short-eared owl feeds heavily on meadow voles, in addition to mice, shrews, rats, and small birds. William Brewster discovered a colony of owls on Muskeget Island off Nantucket, Massachusetts that preyed on terns. He found more than a hundred bodies, all of which had only the breasts picked out.

Paul Roberts and his wife, Julie, both talented birders, once

SHORT-EARED OWL   Photo by Kenneth W. Gardiner.

watched owls on the hunt in Massachusetts. "One Sunday morning," he recalls, "we drove along a road that ran the length of a
salt marsh. Two short-eared owls quickly drew out attention, hunting quite close to the road. On several occasions they flew low over
our car.

"The loping, moth-like flight of the first short-eared captivated us.
With surprising grace and agility, the bird moved quickly over the
dunes at the edge of the marsh. The owl's large head kept shifting left
and right; the bird was hunting with great intensity. Suddenly, its
wings rose well above the horizontal and the owl plummeted feet-first
into the grass, not far from our car. Standing frozen in the grass for
only a second, the owl just as suddenly arose with a meadow vole in
its talons. Swiftly, the owl flew across the marsh to a clump of bay-
berry bushes nestled in a hollow.

"Straining to avoid the curvature of the windshield, through which
I had observed the demise of the rodent, I saw the owl, with vole in
tow, drop into the shrubs. Again, the bird flew up abruptly, as
though jerked by taut strings from above. The short-eared had been
in good view in those bushes, and I had not seen the mouse raised to

the beak, but neither was the vole in its talons now. That recently departed rodent had been cached!

"We saw at least eleven different short-eareds in the marsh that day, but none as well as the superb hunter who caught two mice within fifty yards of our car in less than half an hour."

The owls generally hunt on cloudy days, late afternoons, and at night, gliding and flapping low over the grass. They also keep watch from fence posts, dead trees, and tufts of grass. Birds sleep communally in wintertime, and hunt separately a mile or two from the day-time roost, which may comprise fifty or more owls.

Shortears are gentle, almost tame, but there are always deviants. Charles Urner reported in Bent of a bird that attacked him repeatedly shortly after he imitated a shorebird's calls: "Suddenly a short-eared owl came out of the growing darkness and dove at my straw hat. He missed it by inches. I whistled the yellow-legs call again. He turned and dove at me the second time with no end of determination in his manner. Six times I whistled and six times he swooped at me, finally alighting on a mud pile nearby to look the situation over more carefully. I stood in the open marsh with no protection. Had I whistled in the daylight, he would have shown no interest. Apparently he did not recognize me as a human in the dusk."

Male birds perform spectacular spring flights to attract mates. Seldom seen, these twilight displays involve repeated diving and low tooting noises. Francis Harper was fortunate to see one of their rituals from Gardiners Island, New York: "Late in the afternoon I noticed one of the owls high up in the air, flying with exceptionally slow and somewhat jerky wing strokes at the rate of 150 a minute, and making scarcely any headway. Now and then the bird would swoop downward, meanwhile striking its long wings beneath its body, perhaps eight or twelve times in a second or two. It was a remarkable act, quite unlike anything known to me among other birds. The owl kept more or less over a particular part of the pasture, and was probably 200 or even 300 feet in the air at times."

The shortear is one of the few owls that builds its own nest, although it's no lofty castle. It's a mere depression in the ground, lined with a few blades of grass or weeds, and hidden by surrounding clumps of vegetation. Nests are built in grassy marshes, and are sometimes reused a second year.

An average of from five to seven eggs are deposited in April or May. Incubation takes three weeks. Adults with either eggs or owlets go into a wounded-bird act if intruded upon. Ruses include lame fluttering in the air, wing-flapping (loud for a normally quiet flyer), and crying in distress. If, for example, a raccoon prowls by, the brooding bird might limp off the nest, uttering a squeal like a mouse until the raccoon pursues it. The nest would then be safe. Even fledglings play tricks; when stalked in the open, they roll over and feign death.

Wetlands, whether marsh, swamp, or bog, are vital resources that supply and purify water, and also provide flood control and wildlife habitats. At least 45 million acres (or one-third) of America's original wetlands have been excavated or filled in. Short-eared owls and northern harriers, which inhabit such areas, are gradually disappearing in the muddy wake of backhoes and steam shovels. Wetlands devoid of marsh hawks and marsh owls are less diversified and less interesting places to tramp through.

LONG-EARED OWL

Photo by Herman Weissberg.

Chapter 23

LONG-EARED OWL

Asio otus

Introductory Remarks

The long-eared owl is slim, crow-sized, and wears two ear tufts that rise close together. It is secretive and strictly nocturnal, therefore easily overlooked.

Anyone with luck on their side, however, might run into this species, as Phebe Lewan told the author: "Novice birders *can* have success finding owls. As housewives with spare time and a budding interest in birds, my friend and I sat over a cup of coffee one January morning, deciding on a likely spot for owls in our part of suburban New Jersey. The chosen place, an acre of pine woods with a farm nearby, was not far from home, and off we went with brand new field guides and binoculars. We were barely into the small woods when we saw a shadow overhead — so very silently and quickly — flying between the trees — that landed on a branch just ten feet away. Our first owl! And so close!

"A look in the field guide told us it was a long-eared owl. We were recovering from the combined thrill of seeing an owl and correctly identifying it, when a second one appeared and perched near the first. We were their main interest and they stared at us with golden eyes for a long time. It was hard to leave our first owls, but reciprocal staring can last only so long. We picked up some of their pellets and reluctantly left the woods."

Observation Guidelines

The long-ear breeds sporadically north of Virginia to Canada, and winters in somewhat larger numbers south to Georgia. Largely unnoticed, it was, however, more common in the past. It is a bird of mixed woods, thickets, and especially conifer groves, preferring drier areas than the great horned owl, which it resembles.

The long-ear shows a chestnut face and a streaked, mottled brown breast unlike the horned owl's cross-barred breast. The flight of the long-ear connotes hesitancy as it dodges the evergreens, wafted by buoyant wings.

Although generally the strong, silent type, individual birds can let loose various noises, particularly if disturbed. Its most commonly heard hoot is a single, low Hoo! that resembles a mourning dove's coo, though not as airy. There's also no cadence to the hooting (like barred or horned owls), just a soft call every few seconds. Around the nest, long-ears whine like cats, bark like dogs, and moan like ghosts — the latter notes sounding so unearthly that uninitiated campers tend to peer into the night and wonder why they came.

Natural History

Scientist Alexander Wetmore, while collecting mammals for the U.S. National Museum (now the Smithsonian Institution), once noticed that some of his traps were missing. He later found a long-eared owl nest in a willow tree. The traps lay nearby. Apparently the owls fed on the trapped mice and discarded the traps in wolverine fashion.

Long-ears feed mainly on meadow voles, white-footed mice, and shrews. They also take birds such as sparrows, blackbirds, and evening-singing thrushes, but because the owls are so nocturnal, they don't catch many. Most of the birds that *are* killed are preyed upon during the summer.

These owls are known for their aggressive, demonstrative defense of the young. They exhibit the wounded-bird act like their short-eared cousins; they snap beaks and mew like hungry alley cats, and they've even been seen diving to the ground as if hunting, complete with mimicked cries of the wounded. Of all their routines, however, the most common is also the most startling. A defending owl lowers its swaying head to within inches of its feet, and spreads its wings behind the back to display the outer feathers. Birds in such a threatening pose appear grotesque as well as comical.

When roosting in daytime, especially when strange-looking animals, like humans, are prowling around, they elongate their slender bodies to cylindrical shapes with three-inch diameters. These postures serve as camouflage; the motionless birds look like dead stubs on a branch.

Long-ears rarely make their own nests; they often commandeer a crow, hawk, or red squirrel nest and line it lightly with grass, leaves, feathers, or green twigs. They have also been known to nest inside trees, atop broken stubs, and on the ground. Coniferous forests are usually preferred, and if trees are scarce, they sometimes bunch up in colonies. A dozen birds have been seen together in a small cedar grove, all incubating or brooding.

In late March, and on through April, four to six white, oval eggs are laid, every other day, and incubated by the female for three weeks. During this period, she stays put on the nest. Her mate brings food at night, and she generally won't rise even if the nest tree is disturbed.

The owlets, ugly and old-looking before their time, forsake the nest about a month after hatching — weeks before they can fly. For the next month they flutter from limb to limb on the nest tree, and are fed and guarded by both parents. Family groups stay together through autumn. After the last Indian Summer days are gone, and winter's chill slows the cricket's song to a sputter, some families disband. Others stick together and join other families to eke out an existence on frozen wintering grounds.

Of the more common owls in the East, this species is usually the most difficult to spot. Only patient, experienced birders can hope to find one, unless Lady Luck tags along, as in Phebe Lewan's case. But a few days (and nights) spent in the Great North Woods, with senses alert, should produce either a glimpse of one, or a scream that haunts later dreams.

GREAT HORNED OWL

Photo © by Leonard Lee Rue III.

Chapter 24

GREAT HORNED OWL

Bubo virginianus

Introductory Remarks

Also known as the cat owl and tiger of the air, the great horned is the largest common owl in the East, and has two-inch ear tufts and a white throat.

Up until 1965, the state of Pennsylvania paid five dollar bounties for each horned owl scalp, and although fully protected by state and federal laws today, the species still gets shot at nationwide by accident or from spite. It takes some game animals, thus garnering hunters' wrath. Owls are best left alone, as an event near Keene, New Hampshire in January 1982 demonstrates. A great horned owl flew into the windshield of a mail truck and landed between the cab and the trailer. The bird managed to free itself in Keene while police ran around for the next hour trying to capture it. When New Hampshire Audubon staff members joined in the chase, the dazed owl was soon overtaken and brought to Willard Pond Sanctuary in Antrim. After being examined and cared for, the bird was released when the weather warmed.

Observation Guidelines

Horned owls are fairly common residents throughout North America — the widest range of any owl. They are non-migratory, but birds of the extreme North withdraw a bit in winter. Normally thought of as owls of deep woods, they also range across open country, and are doing well near the city, where they subsist on rats, pigeons, and an occasional stray cat.

These four-pound predators have white throats and barred brown underparts. They appear to be neckless. Females, which are larger than males, reach two feet tall with a wingspread of almost five feet. Their talons lock after sinking into flesh; in one case, a biologist whose hand was impaled by a captive bird had to cut the owl's leg tendons to free himself.

Calls are low, muffled hoots in a series of five or seven, the last two being more emphatic. Even in a dense forest, when the hoots sound like they're delivered through a mitten, the calls carry well, with an urgent, don't-come-near-me tone. When hooting, the owls lean forward, fluff out the white throat feathers, and close the eyes slightly, making the birds look all the more feline. The beak is scarcely opened. From a distance, hooting sounds like the cooing of a dove or the barking of a big dog.

Natural History

The horned owl will hunt anything it can handle, and it can handle surprisingly large prey. Regular items include: rabbits, squirrels, weasels, muskrats and smaller rodents, and skunks. It is one of the few predators that will touch a skunk; apparently the owl doesn't mind the strong smell, but museum curators do when they get a reeking, stuffed specimen. The odor can last for years.

Great horned owls also take birds such as grouse, quail, hawks and owls (including the barred, which is nearly the size of the horned), and several species of waterfowl. In times of plenty, they habitually open up the prey's skull and eat only the brain.

These owls hunt by night but when forced, by day. They are

YOUNG GREAT HORNED OWLS   Photo © by Leonard Lee Rue III.

powerful flyers that can soar like hawks, and have been clocked with a car's speedometer at 40 mph. Attacks on humans are numerous. Most encounters occur when people climb up to inspect their nests, take pictures, or try to band the owlets. A typical confrontation was reported by Arthur Cleveland Bent many years ago. "As I neared the nest," he wrote, "I felt a stunning blow behind my ear, which nearly dazed me, and off sailed my hat a hundred feet away; her sharp talons had struck into my scalp, making two ugly wounds from which the blood flowed freely. This was the limit; I did not care to be scalped or knocked senseless to the ground, so down I came, leaving the owls the masters of the situation."

A more recent attack (December, 1981), totally unprovoked, was reported from Blue Hill, Maine. An owl, apparently disoriented after hitting a house, went after a man and a boy as night was falling. "It was like a magnet sucking right on you," said Jeff Torrey. "It dug its claws in, knocked me four or five feet until I ran into my own fence. I couldn't imagine what the hell it was!" Along with the goshawk, the horned owl is the raptor most likely to injure people. They demand solitude.

Julio de la Torre managed to watch a pair courting in March, 1976, without being noticed. On a full-moon night at Paugussett State Forest, Connecticut, he was sitting above a talus slope overlooking the Housatonic River when he heard a horned owl hoot, then fly across the river toward him. After it alighted in a nearby hemlock, another owl sounded and abruptly perched beside the waiting male. "It was obvious to me," he told the author, "that the two birds had never met. They went berserk with their mating rituals for about 45 minutes. They danced, hooted, purred, headbobbed, and mated three times. During the third session, I actually heard the wings of the male, beating hard to stay atop the female. All the while they were completely oblivious to me.

"Then a new sound came, like human laughter with deep pain — haunted and strange. I thought it was a kid on angel dust! The pair hooted back ferociously and then fled together. It turned out to be the melancholy laugh of a female great horned owl who was trying to entice the already-taken male. I had witnessed a rarely seen, incredible owl love triangle. I still can't believe it to this day."

Pairs normally court in January or early February, resulting in females incubating during late-winter snowstorms. The birds reuse old hawk, crow, or squirrel nests, adding nothing but a few feathers. They favor the center of secluded woodlots and readily appropriate those nests located in white pines. Dr. Louis Bishop found that the adult owls he studied in Connecticut destroyed their own nests as soon as the young could step up in the tree crotch, thus making the young less conspicuous to roving crows.

Two or three eggs are laid before spring. Within two weeks of hatching, the chicks are one-third adult size, wearing thick buff-colored down. At a month they are half grown, with the partially developed wings and the tail feathers peeking out of the sheaths. It was at this stage that Barbara Gard, while birdbanding at Manomet Bird Observatory in Massachusetts, had a first-hand experience with great horned owls. In the spring of 1981, a young owl was found in a cemetery and brought in. Gard and other interns banded and force-fed it, and then another owlet was brought in. Three days later, the interns took them back to the cemetery and placed them in the nest, which was about 40 feet up in a pine. Gard and company had their hands full, as the young birds wouldn't stay put and the parents frequently divebombed, keeping active even by day.

For the next two weeks, Gard found the young birds farther and farther away from the nest, but each day she put them back in the tree, receiving thanks in the form of owl hisses. On her last day at the cemetery she saw no owls. Later, she marvelled at the parents, for they had continued to feed the young regardless of their being handled daily and having been away from home for several days.

Great horned owls exude authority and vigor when seen up close, but their presence can be felt a mile away when the somber hoots weave through the woods on a quiet evening.

BARRED (or hoot) OWL

Photo by Henry B. Kane.

Chapter 25

BARRED OWL

Strix varia

Introductory Remarks

This is the only large, dark, brown-eyed owl in the East.

Known in different regions as the hoot or swamp owl, the barred owl is probably the most vocal and inquisitive of all, responding to any half-hearted mimicked hoots. As author-naturalist Donald Stokes says, "It's not very hard to fool an owl." This is especially true of *Strix varia*.

From the 1960s to the present, barred owls have extended their range dramatically in the West, along the U.S.-Canadian border. Before 1965 they were unknown in the Pacific Northwest, but now are local breeders. It will be interesting to see which species wins out there — the barred or the closely related, but rare spotted owl, since their ranges have only recently overlapped.

Observation Guidelines

The barred owl is rather common throughout the East and as far north as James Bay. It is uncommon, however, on Cape Cod and Long Island, where there's a scarcity of swamps or wet woods. Birds winter on the Massachusetts and New York coastal plains, but they don't breed there. They are permanent residents over the rest of the range.

Look for this species in low, moist woods, river bottoms, and wooded swamps. Wherever red-shouldered hawks live, barred owls should also be found, and in greater numbers. The hawks are active by day and the owls hunt at night with little conflict, and sometimes both species use the same nest in alternate years.

This is a round-headed owl with bars across the chest, contrasting with the streaking below. Overall, it is a stocky, gray-brown bird standing almost two feet tall.

The barred owl is noisy year-round, but especially so in February and March, when pairs perform hooting duets that make quite a racket. The most commonly heard pattern consists of eight hoots in two sets of four, sounding like: Hoo, hoo, ho-ho...hoo, hoo, ho-ho-aw! The extra syllable, "aw," which drops off at the end of the pattern, is diagnostic. Hoots are clear, emphatic, and sound very similar to a baying dog at a half-mile, but the rhythmic pattern cannot be mistaken. Other whoops and jabberings can be heard, in addition to a rising, plaintive scream that, at the end, sounds more like a cat than any owl. Many of the varied calls are unnerving, and although the owls do most of their hooting in early evening and just before dawn, campers can be awakened at all hours.

Natural History

Throughout most of its range, the barred owl feeds on mice, birds, insects, and mammals up to the size of opossums. In Florida, however, it specializes in fish, crayfish, crabs, water rats, and the destructive cotton rats that cause serious damage to southern crops.

When winter's snow hides the rodents that tunnel within, quieting their footfalls, some owls wind up in cities where they eat well but have to deal with people taking their pictures. In 1977, for example, a bird spent the Christmas season lurking around Boston's Gardner Museum and Fine Arts Museum, feasting in style on abundant rats and gray squirrels.

BARRED OWL   Photo by Neal Clark.

The barred owl is essentially submissive and unaggressive. It steers clear of horned owls, but will fight nomadic goshawks to the death, and often kills screech owls. Physical contact with humans is rare.

On late-winter nights, pairs sing chuckling duets, interspersed with boisterous calls of Wha, wha, ho-ho! They bob and weave on their perches, singing for hours. Of all eastern owls, the barred is probably the easiest to observe courting, because they don't seem to mind an audience.

When they nest, they usually choose a tree cavity or reuse a crow or red-shouldered hawk nest. They favor cavities with depths of two feet or more. Northern birds nest in white pines and hemlocks; southern birds nest in mixed or deciduous woods, often consisting of willows, sycamores, red maples, or cottonwoods.

Barred owls grow attached to their nesting sites, as evidenced by Arthur Cleveland Bent's records in Massachusetts. He kept track of two nests for 26 to 33 consecutive years apiece, and while checking one of them, almost died. "I shinned the old trunk without my climbers," he wrote, "and, in reaching into the deep cavity for the eggs, I slipped and my arm became tightly wedged in the narrow slit at the lower end of the opening. I struggled hopelessly for 25 minutes (by the village clock), calling in vain for help, before I finally tore my arm loose and dropped exhausted to the ground." Because of this mishap, his finger nerves were permanently damaged and from then on he wrote with a trembling hand.

The usual clutch size is two, but sometimes three, eggs, which are dull white and typically laid in March. Both parents incubate for almost a month. Nests, already a year or two old when the owls appropriate them, can be death traps for the birds due to the flattened, worn out condition. Eggs and owlets often roll out, yet the young can survive falls of 40 feet or more. Parents care for the offspring through the first summer, tearing up chunks of meat and feeding them, and later teaching them to fly and hunt for themselves. Come fall, the parents coolly turn their backs; the immature owls are then on their own.

Barred owls, with their big heads, dark eyes, and humorous, baritone voices, are strangely human. Nevertheless, adequate information about their habits is lacking because it is so difficult (and often soggy) to locate nesting sites. What is known is this: They need standing deadwood — or, snags — to breed. Traditionally, foresters have culled dead and dying trees out of mature stands because snags have minimal commercial value and tend to harbor disease.

Due to even-aged management (cutting trees of the same age), clear-cutting, and burning wood for heat, standing deadwood is becoming scarce in many areas of this country. As Henry Laramie, a New Hampshire Fish and Game official, said recently, "There is a definite shortage of den trees, and it's becoming more acute all the time."

Snags are paradise to denning mammals and cavity-nesting birds.

The spotted owl of the West requires dense, mature groves of trees at least 200 years old. Its prime habitat is falling at an alarming rate. The eastern barred owl, common and safe for now, could imperceptibly disappear if deadwood is not left standing for wildlife.

BARN OWL

Photo by Henry B. Kane.

Chapter 26

BARN OWL

Tyto alba

Introductory Remarks

This is a striking, pale bird — the only owl with a heart-shaped face. The genus name, *Tyto,* is derived from the Greek for night owl; the species name, *alba,* means white.

During the 12th century, the Tartars attributed the saving of Genghis Khan's life to the barn owl. The famous conqueror once had his horse shot from under him in battle, and because the fight was going badly, he ran and hid in a thicket. When his pursuers followed, they confronted an owl sitting over the hiding Khan. They immediately gave up the search.

In the 20th century, changes wrought by man have severely affected this owl here and in Europe. Mechanized farming practices meant fewer horses, which in turn meant less grain for rodents to eat, hence fewer barn owls. DDT took a heavy toll on both continents, and the owls also made easy targets for gunners because they breed so close to people, they quarter low over the ground, and their light color really stands out. The current problem that these owls face is a scarcity of nesting sites. Airy old barns are tumbling, and even church towers — long-time favorite haunts — are no longer available because most are boarded up to prevent pigeons from entering. Because of this site scarcity, the barn owl is on the National Audubon Society's Blue List of declining species.

Observation Guidelines

Although barn owls find extreme cold forbidding and sometimes fatal, they have expanded their range northward during this century. They are found on every continent in the world. In the eastern United States, birds are largely permanent residents from New York State and Massachusetts south to Florida, and are irregular visitors to northern New England. They're also rare in the Appalachians.

Paul Stewart conducted a study in the 1950s on 336 banded specimens, and discovered that birds north of Georgia were migratory (moving 100 miles or more), while more southern birds tended to stay put year-round. He also found a marked difference in longevity of the owls in the two regions: northern birds lived shorter lives, no doubt caused by migratory hazards.

Barn owls are local breeders in open country, farmland, and around towns. If left alone, they raise young in the midst of civilization; pairs bred in the northeast tower of the old Smithsonian building in Washington, D.C., for a hundred consecutive years. A pair also nested in a church steeple in Berkeley, California for several years. Because of the owl's nocturnal habits, though, most people never get to know their raptor neighbors.

Barn owls are dark-eyed, long-legged birds of prey. Their backs are buffy brown and their underparts are a striking white, liberally speckled with dark spots. When seen flying on moonlit nights, deeply beating their long wings, they conjure up thoughts of ghosts on a shivering Halloween.

If any species is named the screech owl, this should be the one, for it emits high, raspy screams that sound like a woman finding a corpse in the closet. These screeches are blood-curdling and fill the night air with a charged-up tension. Naturalists are enchanted, savoring every

BARN OWL WITH PREY   Photo © by Leonard Lee Rue III.

discordant note, while those unfamiliar with the monkey-faced owl simply cower. Other calls include snores, grunts, and loud feline hisses.

Natural History

Barn owls feed almost exclusively on various species of mice, rats, and squirrels, along with a few birds. In the West they take scores of pocket gophers, to the glee of farmers. They spend more time actively hunting than any other owl.

In the early 1960s, Roger Payne investigated the barn owl's use of hearing in locating prey. At about the same time, the Massachusetts Audubon Society conducted experiments in totally dark rooms. Barn owls were able to catch mice running around on dead leaves time after time. In 1981, Eric Knudsen, a professor of neurobiology at Stanford University, California did further investigations, concluding that barn owls can locate prey by sound alone; they can locate sounds of the horizontal and vertical dimensions better than any other animal tested; and while hunting, these birds cover more area than any other nocturnal bird. (One-hundred-acre hunting ranges are usual.)

The barn owl's special hearing method involves a big round face made of tightly-packed feathers that reflect and amplify high-frequency sounds — like cupped hands around human ears. Each of its ears is set at a different angle; the right ear is angled slightly upward to catch sounds from above, while the left ear, according to Knudsen, is angled down to catch sounds from below. The owl's brain then interprets the auditory information it receives, enabling the bird to strike.

Shunning daylight, the barn owl is active during the dark hours when it hunts on silent, weaving wings. Its only enemies are great horned owls and men. Olive Rhines, who cared for countless orphan birds during her 25 years of service with the Connecticut Audubon Society, once had a couple of these owls brought to her. "They were dutifully fed," she told the author, "under protest to the last, with rodents supplemented by liver and hamburg. The owls remained fierce and untamable. They hissed menacingly at my approach, sweeping their chins back and forth on the floor, their talons ready to strike out. It took some nerve to grasp them by their legs and stuff their mouths with chunks of meat. More than once I emerged from the feeding session with bleeding hands."

There are two unusual characteristics about this raptor: It is capable of breeding year-round, and when food is scarce they produce fewer offspring. In the South, evidence points to two broods — a rarity among birds of prey. The state of New York has egg records from July to December, and Washington, D.C., reports that eggs are commonly laid in April.

Barn owls often nest in man-made structures, including barns, steeples, abandoned mines and wells, silos, and even duck blinds. They also take to natural sites such as tree cavities, underground burrows, and the sides of cliffs.

The owls don't build nests, instead depositing the five to nine eggs on top of accumulated pellets. More than most owls, their white eggs are nearly oval, not round. Within a month of the first egg laid (they're laid at intervals of two to three days), the oldest owlet hatches, often weeks before the youngest. In another couple of months the owlets fledge, spreading out over the countryside.

The season is winter. The setting is a weathered steeple high above a peaceful village. A biting wind forces tattered louvers into creaking complaints. Inside, a dry, musty smell lingers close. Six long-beaked barn owls huddle on their ancestral roost, as evidenced by the mat of glazed, black pellets a foot thick. Bills snapping, they back up against a yellowed wall, swaying their hung heads and rocking their tawny bodies in unison. The owls are safe here as long as churches provide sanctuary for both bird and man.

SAW-WHET OWL

Chapter 27

SAW-WHET OWL

Aegolius acadicus

Introductory Remarks

The saw-whet owl, only the size of a bluebird, is the smallest owl in the East. The species name, *acadicus,* refers to Acadia, the wild region of the Northeast which spills over into present-day Nova Scotia.

This owl, although timid, is tolerant of man almost to the point of tameness. There are many accounts of people touching and banding these birds, then placing them back on the same branch. Such tameness could be dismissed as a trusting nature, but it really borders on stupidity. (A captive owl once failed to recognize liver as meat, and only when the meat was stuffed inside a mouse skin did the bird feed.) Because of their size, few owls are shot, but many are killed by cars each year.

Observation Guidelines

The saw-whet owl is a permanent resident from Canada to Pennsylvania, and wintering birds wander as far south as Tennessee. Its breeding status remains uncertain in many locations due to its size and shyness, but the species is probably more common than it is thought to be. State Audubon societies need more volunteers who are willing to participate in Breeding Bird Atlas projects that establish numbers and distributions of all birds in each state. Maryland was the first to begin such a survey in 1971, Massachusetts completed their five-year study in 1980, and New Hampshire started theirs in 1981. Projects such as these, where participants regularly scour their assigned two-square-mile territories, can answer questions about a species' breeding status, including the whereabouts of this elfin owl.

Saw-whet owls hide in honeysuckle thickets, coniferous forests, and isolated pine groves. In winter they come out of their shells a bit, visiting barns, porches, and watching birdfeeders for easy prey. One of the best ways to detect them is by searching likely areas during daylight and listening for chickadees who scold the roosting owls. Chickadees are notorious for hounding the saw-whets unmercifully with harsh calls of Dee dee dee! In doing so, they give the owls away to the delight of hard-pressed birders.

At close range, adults show a blotchy brown head and a black beak. Underparts are white and brown, almost rufous. Juvenile birds are more chocolate brown, with prominent white eyebrows. Size alone can identify this species, for no other owl in the East is barely the size of a person's fist. Unlike the larger screech owl, saw-whets lack ear tufts. They fly quickly and easily, zigzagging through heavy timber just like a woodcock. When taking off from a perch, they tend to descend straight down before flying forward.

Calls resemble a crosscut saw being sharpened — a series of excited whistled notes that sound more like an insect singing than an owl calling. The notes come out in rapid succession and are difficult to describe, let alone imitate. Saw-whets also coo and hiss, but except during late winter and early spring, they are silent.

In March, 1982, a person in South Sutton, New Hampshire heard a beeping noise and thought it was a distress signal from a downed airplane. He called the state police, and when the policeman entered the woods with a flashlight, a "big bird" flew off. Area birders agreed that

SAW-WHET OWLS

Photo courtesy of Maine Department of Inland Fisheries and Wildlife.

it was a saw-whet owl that only seemed big in the middle of the night.

Natural History

Saw-whet owls kill mice, chipmunks, bats, and sometimes animals larger than themselves like squirrels and rats. There is a gruesome account in Bent's *Life Histories* series about a Mr. Cutting of Lyme, New Hampshire who was plagued by one of these harmless-looking birds: "He had 25 pigeons that roosted nightly on perches in his barn. The dove-hole was close by in the barn door. Seven pigeons lay dead one morning on the hay beneath their perches. The birds' heads were gone, some feathers were lying about, and there was some blood on their bodies; otherwise there was no sign. The following evening Mr. Cutting went by stealth into his barn. By the light of his lantern he found two more headless pigeons on the hay. Looking up he saw the killer perched on a beam. He dispatched it with a long stick."

Ken Rubin, a city forester in Queens, New York encountered an owl roosting peacefully at the nearby Jamaica Bay Wildlife Refuge in January, 1982. "The owl sat," he wrote the author, "in a sheltered area of eastern red cedars and American hollies. It was perched in the holly and I was able to get within three feet. It didn't look real. It looked like a toy that you could take home with you. I thought its eyes were closed when all of a sudden this tiny head swiveled, and two big yellow eyes met mine."

Paul Roberts, similarly, met one of these birds face to face: "One March day, Julie, my wife, and I were walking in thick pine woods. We had been searching for crossbills, grosbeaks, and boreal chickadees, but without success, so we decided to stretch out in a protected clearing, soak up the sun, and take a luxurious nap. As we lay on the bed of pine needles, I looked up into the pine tree in front of us. The shadows of the branches created an odd image on the trunk. I turned to Julie and said, 'The way the sun is filtering through the pine branches, it looks like there's a saw-whet owl sitting on that branch.' Julie looked up, laughed, and agreed, 'It really does.' We talked further, but as the sun temporarily moved behind the clouds, I noticed the shadow on the tree didn't change. I stood up to examine this unusual shadow more carefully. Of course it was a saw-whet owl, with one eye open. It had been watching us all the time."

These birds can be captured by hand, as seen by Major Bendire's report in Bent: "I have also found them equally stupid in the vicinity of Camp Harney, Oregon. Each winter one or more specimens were brought to me alive by some of my men, who found them sitting in the shrubbery bordering a creek directly in the rear of their quarters, where they usually allowed themselves to be taken without making any effort to escape. I thought at first that they were possibly starved, and on that account too weak to fly, but on examination found them mostly in good condition and fairly fat."

Saw-whet owls nest inside dead trees, often via an abandoned woodpecker hole. They also accept birdhouses, as the Massachusetts Audubon Society recently demonstrated. Four to six pure white eggs are laid inside a cavity, with no lining except some wood chips. In the South, eggs are laid in late March or April, while in the Northeast, they're laid in April or May. Incubating birds are not easily disturbed; they can be lifted off by hand, but only birdbanders should make such assaults.

The best way to locate one of these owls is to knock on wood. That is, look for old flicker holes with diameters of three inches or more, and gently rap on likely nesting trees. An owl is bound to poke its head out (filling the entrance), to see who the uninvited guest is. Whoever comes to the front door, be it a saw-whet owl, a more reticent screech owl, or a flying squirrel, it'll be in a sour mood, so expect a leery look.

BURROWING OWL   Photo by Kenneth W. Gardiner.

Chapter 28

BURROWING OWL

Athene cunicularia

Introductory Remarks

Short but long-legged, the burrowing owl is the only owl that lives on the ground. The genus name, *Athene,* honors the daughter of Zeus, protectress of Athens. The species name, *cunicularia,* is Latin for miner or burrower.

Misguided government officials and farmers have indirectly persecuted burrowing owls out West since the 1800s, and the killing still goes on. The problem is that the owls happen to nest in prairie dog burrows, and these rodents compete with cattle for grasses. In addition, the burrows can break a cow's or horse's legs if stepped in. To keep the ranchers happy, the Bureau of Sport Fisheries and Wildlife threw cyanide cartridges down the burrows or simply sealed them up. If that didn't work, they laced oats with Compound 1080, a cheap, yet deadly, long-lasting chemical that doesn't readily break down in the soil. As a result, unsuspecting owls feeding on tainted corpses were also poisoned.

Although 1080 was banned in 1972, ranchers who are troubled by coyotes want to see it made available again. Much of the sheep and cattle raising is done on public domain, and this is where the poisoning still occurs. In 1980, the National Park Service, pressured by ranchers whose land abuts Badlands National Park in South Dakota, planned to poison thirteen prairie dog colonies inside park boundaries. Personnel proposed to use zinc phosphide, a persistent chemical which is toxic to anything that moves. It will be a head-hanging day when the National Park Service — normally an ecologically aware agency — succumbs to outside pressures and purposely kills wildlife that it's been protecting since the National Park Service Act of 1916.

Observation Guidelines

In 1966 the U.S. Department of the Interior classified the burrowing owl as "rare." In 1973 it was listed as "status undetermined," meaning the species could be rare or merely uncommon, but no one knew for sure. Ten years later, the bird's status is still unknown, especially in the West where it breeds locally in the remaining prairies and open grasslands. In the East, only Florida supports breeding populations, but there, especially in the northern part of the state, owls are increasing.

Individual birds occasionally straggle as far as New England; in 1980 there was a rash of sightings in coastal Connecticut and Massachusetts. In May, 1978, a hardy bird made it to the Isles of Shoals off New Hampshire, but a ship-assisted passage cannot be ruled out since Portsmouth Harbor is less than ten miles away.

In the Sunshine State, the owls occupy cattle country, prairies, and vacant lots. Uncultivated, level ground is preferred, but when lacking, birds resort to nesting along airports and railroad right-of-ways. Golfers sometimes even spot these comical owls bowing up and down on their own small-scale bunkers.

Burrowing owls are barely the size of pigeons, with long legs, stubby tails, and an overall mottled brown appearance. They also sport white chin stripes and seem to frown much of the time. They fly as little as possible.

The birds make two distinct calls: a chuckle or cackle while flying, and a rich, double-noted cooing on spring nights. The latter calls sound very much like a miniature train tooting.

Natural History

Out West, the owls favor scorpions, beetles, and pocket mice, but in Florida they eat many crustaceans (crabs and their kin), fish, snakes, and an assortment of insects.

They hunt mostly at night, but remain active during the day, when they are seen perched on fence posts or the ground. Flights are short, undulating, and include hovering. The pioneering conservationist, Aldo Leopold, wrote about their curious habit of following large animals: "It made a daily practice of 'pursuing' a bird dog when the dog was turned loose for exercise near the golf links of the Albuquerque Country Club. When the dog first appeared on the owl's range, he would chase the owl for a short distance. When this was over, the owl would chase him for distances up to 150 yards, flying about five feet behind and above him as the dog hunted." Perhaps the owls benefit by anything rustled up by all the commotion.

In Florida, where prairie dogs are absent, owls nest in gopher tortoise burrows or in extensive underground armadillo dens. Unlike western birds, the Florida birds seem capable of digging their own holes, using beaks and feet. Eastern birds also tend to be less colonial on breeding grounds. In the Old West, when prairie dog towns sprawled for hundreds of square miles across the plains, burrowing owls bred in adjacent colonies of their own.

The burrows are often ten feet long and only one or two feet deep because Florida's water table is so close to ground level. The six to eight eggs are deposited on a mat of dry manure or grass in early spring. Both parents incubate and guard against predators such as skunks, opossums, and pigmy rattlesnakes.

These tame, whimsical raptors, when closely approached, demonstrate a variety of odd postures. Sometimes they stand stiffly at attention on one leg. Sometimes they bob their heads in unison, and at other times they just glare back intently. Try as they may, none of these tricks is effective at scaring people away. We're more apt to giggle.

LONG-EARED OWL

Photo courtesy of Maine Department of
Inland Fisheries and Wildlife.

Chapter 29

THE NATURAL MYSTERY OF OWLING

In the 18th century, an owler was a smuggler of sheep or wool from England to France. A few years later it meant a person who sat up all night, now called a nightowl. But an owler today is a daring birder who stalks nocturnally. Members of this spirited breed often go alone, either because they prefer doing it solo, or because everyone else is sleeping; there aren't many folks who enjoy standing around gloomy woods listening for somber owl hoots.

But the number of owlers is increasing. Julio de la Torre, from Connecticut, has led more than 10,000 people on assorted owl prowls around New England since 1972. He himself can't get enough of it. "I'll spend eight hours at a time in the woods," he said, "sitting in one spot listening for owls, and be perfectly happy. I guess I'm a good yoga man."

Sometimes, though, he gets more than he bargains for: He's been strafed by a pair of marauding screech owls while trying to lead a group of 40 children, and had an owl fly in and out of his car. A barred owl once attacked him, missed his head by inches, then perched two feet above, hooting in his face. His obsession with nocturnal birding has taken him from Florida to Nova Scotia in his endless quest to record, photograph, and admire the mysterious winged wildlife in the dead of night.

Professor Robert Vernon is also wild about owls, heading for darkened woodlots around Boston whenever he gets the chance. "Owls are rather stand-offish," he says, "and very majestic — almost romantic — creatures of the night." At the Hale Reservation in his home town of Westwood, Massachusetts, he once imitated a great horned owl by voice. "I was at the edge of a small pond," he recalls, "and nearby lived the caretaker. After two or three hoots by me, I heard a truck door slam, engine rev up, and then a pickup truck raced down the hill. He had a search light and he shined his beam over my way. I was behind a few trees or he would have seen me for sure. I'm convinced that he thought I was an owl, and I was flattered, as the owls themselves did not seem to take me seriously."

In 1972, on a night hike led by Dr. Arthur Borror of the University of New Hampshire, I rekindled my own interest in owls. An hour before that spring dawn, a dozen of us students stopped prowling to huddle beneath moonlit shade-trees. Some had eyes skyward, some looked to the ground, and the rest of us whispered in anticipation. Borror then turned away from us, cupped his large hands around his mouth, and barked out two sets of canine howls, the last syllable ending in a lower-pitched, "Awhh!" A few students snickered, but most were all ears for the unknown.

Within minutes, as if on cue, two brownish birds suddenly landed fifteen feet over Borror's tall figure, returning his mimicked hoots and more — emitting wails and monkey-like jabbering that made a hideous racket. The owls' dark eyes probed. After floating from oak to oak, bowing and swaying all the while and circling around the captive audience, the barred owls abruptly drifted away into the surrounding gloom. Silence. A few seconds later our sleepy, spellbound group erupted, creating a din of joy. We knew that we had just witnessed a special performance, but we also knew that there'd be no encores that night. It was getting light.

While caretaking at a private school in Chestnut Hill, Massachusetts, I was awakened at 2:30 one summer morn by low, faraway hoots of two great horned owls. When I bolted up and looked out the window, I was amazed to see them perched side by side on the school's golden beaver weathervane. When I really came to and managed to shine a flashlight on them, they vanished over the roof. Repeated attempts at drawing them back by playing recorded hoots out the window failed. Just a couple of days before, I had found a three-inch owl pellet on the campus, composed mostly of pigeon feathers. The irony was that I had spent much of the previous winter hanging around frigid woods only a half-mile away trying to chase down this wary species that I *knew* was there, only to have dreams shattered that August morning by a muffled, "Hoo, hoo, hooo...ho, ho!"

Pellets, or castings, are matted balls of indigestible bone, fur, and hair that are regurgitated eight to twelve hours after swallowing. Raptors, crows, gulls, herons, and other birds which prey on vertebrates all cough them up — a process taking about five minutes, culminating with a wet, glistening object being expelled from an incredibly wide-open mouth. The larger the bird, the larger the pellet, thus the great horned owl ejects pellets up to four inches long, while the screech owl puts out one-inchers. Hawk pellets tend to be composed of fur or feathers, due to the birds' habit of tearing morsels from the bone, whereas owls, who gobble down whole prey, make pellets loaded with bones. Entire rodent skulls often pass intact. With practice, anyone can identify exactly what the bird ate by checking the size and shape of skulls, as well as dental formulae.

Night-owling isn't for everyone. It takes nerve. But those who brave the obscure world of darkness discover that their senses are better than expected; acute enough to distinguish a barred owl from a barking dog at a mile; acute enough to tell a screech owl from a big brown bat coursing through a lifeless cemetery; and acute enough to *feel* a horned owl's commanding presence.

Thoreau, while at Walden Pond, "...rejoiced that there are owls. Let them do the idiotic and maniacal hooting for men. It is a sound admirably suited to swamps and twilight woods which no day illustrates, suggesting a vast and undeveloped nature which men have not recognized." The night world is a different world, still unexplored and unknown. It's a realm of heavy odors, vague shapes, and penetrating noises. As Ambrose Bierce wrote in one of his weird tales, "The very silence has another quality than the silence of the day. And it is full of half-heard whispers — whispers that startle — ghosts of sounds long dead."

Winter nights, however, with a full moon shining on snow, seem almost as bright as day. A trip to a snowy pasture at such a time is like sand dunes at dawn: the sky is inky blue, the moon is a squinting white, and the waves of new snow sparkle like mounds of sand. The whirring of the wind through surrounding pines recalls the sound of a spent wave receding at the beach. Animal tracks are erased the next day.

Late winter to early spring is the season to go owling because the birds are courting, mating, and at their loudest. Any time after sunset can be fruitful, although a study conducted in West Virginia in 1975 revealed that a majority of screech owls were attracted after 3 AM. The best plan for successful night-owling is to start during daylight. Comb areas where owls have been reported recently, looking for those pellets under big trees. They show up well on snow. Scan tree trunks and limbs for whitewashing by the birds' feces, and be alert for songbirds squawking.

Paul Roberts was watching a crowd of crows apparently harassing a raptor in Medford, Massachusetts, when, after trying to locate the missing bird, he confronted a great horned owl in a tree ten feet away. "It looked at me with such ferocity," he said, "that I literally shook with fear. We stared at each other for what seemed like ten minutes as the crows slowly tired of their game. They finally gave up and the owl then leaned over and glided away. For me, it was almost a religious experience, because the great horned owl is one of the most awesome birds of prey in the world."

Along with nerve, owling takes patience. As Julio de la Torre says, "For every owl seen, I'll hear about ten." Many nights out are needed to even hear anything, but every night prowl is an adventure that few people experience. I've often spent several consecutive nights in vain, hooting and hoping for hours, only to sulk homeward to the stereo and play the owls' greatest hits. But a strange compulsion grips me time and again, forcing me to return. The reward of finding owls comes only to those who wait.

Anyone wanting to participate should wear warm, dark clothing to provide comfort while standing around and to reduce conspicuousness. Carry a flashlight, but use it sparingly as wildlife is extremely sensitive to light at night. Besides, as tests have proven, humans can, with practice, see better in the blackness than a bear can, and almost as well as a cat. (Our night vision, however, pales compared to that of owls.) Within a half-hour our eyes adjust to the dark, which is rarely pitch black.

Optional equipment includes a compass and binoculars — the glasses helping to zoom in and gather more available starlight bounced off water and snow. Owlers near the city should inform police or landowners of their plans; night-owlers don't cherish being mistaken for night-prowlers.

I sometimes carry a wooden stool to sit on while waiting for something to happen. A lightweight, collapsible seat would be even better. Once, around the witching hour on a teeth-chattering New England night, I was trudging through deep snow toward a lakeside park when I spied a police cruiser idling at the entrance. I tried to slip by, but that was impossible. At six feet, five inches tall, lugging a two-foot high stool, and being the only other person in the vicinity, I more than stood out. I glowed in the dark. So he called me over to his car.

"Excuse me, are you all right?" he asked.

"Oh, sure. I'm just gonna listen for owls out there by the lake," I replied, knowing that I wasn't coming off too well.

"I...see. You sit in the snow listening for birds?" A vacant, disbelieving look crept over his young face.

"Yeah, for owls," I said. "I'm going owling if it's okay with you."

"Go ahead. Just don't freeze to death, jeez!"

With that he rolled up his window and took off, while I headed toward the beckoning shadows that would shelter both an owl and a fugitive nighttime owler.

Instead of roaming the winter woods trying to flush out the owls, it's a good idea to let them come to you. Sit on a hilltop or the edge of a woodlot and be still. Get out the thermos of hot stuff and relax. (Owling is supposed to be fun, after all.) Some owlers play recorded hoots from cassette tape players to attract birds even closer. Barn, barred, screech, and great horned owls are especially curious and respond vocally to mimicked hooting. Owlers using tapes — considered to be cheating by some fellow birders — generally start with a tape of a small owl and work up to the great horned; if they began with a big owl, the smaller species would be afraid to reply. More than once, Boston's Robert Vernon played screech owl calls and had a horned owl answer the magical acetate. A hard-to-obtain tape is that of a dying rabbit. Its cries, which variously sound like a crow cawing or a piglet squealing, work wonders in attracting any owl within range. The using of tapes to lure owls should be kept at a minimum, however, for it interferes with their hunting schedules.

Nighttime without owls would render the woods too quiet, too safe. It does us good to go out there and get goose pimples at the sound of the first hoot. Then we know that we're really living, not just crossing off dull days on the calendar. There's plenty for everyone to learn about the night, and with more than half of the world's creatures active nocturnally, only those persons who sit up with the owls can become complete naturalists.

Epilogue

Of the 26 raptor species covered in this book, no fewer than 15 are currently in trouble or headed in that direction. The loss of quality habitats due to logging, dredging, and urban sprawl takes a heavy toll, forcing the birds to move on to less desirable areas where competition is keener. More than any other group of birds, raptors, as hunters, require acres or even square miles of elbow room. Unfortunately for both birds and people, this elbow room is being altered beyond recognition as we blindly hurtle toward the 21st century. The U.S. Environmental Protection Agency estimates that approximately two million acres are rendered useless to wildlife each year.

Ever since about 1962, when Rachel Carson's *Silent Spring* appeared (the book that attacked the chemical industry, the Department of Agriculture, and industrialization in general), people everywhere have been more aware of their own environment because, as some decorative posters illustrate, "We're all in this together." Carson was called an "hysterical woman" by some complacent officials, but all she did was calmly start the environmental movement, which did us all a world of good.

In the twenty years since her book came out, *we* were the hysterical ones, fleeing the choking cities in droves, and hastening for cleaner, greener retreats that rural America offers. The impact of recent human migration on the raptors' already-precarious existence is sure to be deleterious unless these people develop a sensitivity for wildlife. All life is sacred.

Even sacred federal lands, however, such as National Forests and Parks, are being invaded and desecrated, affecting the success of even attempts to empower the Secretary of the Interior to lease National Park acreage for mining. Many of the 326 units of the National Park System, which encompass over 30 million acres of prime wildlife habitat, are destined for spoilage. Birds of prey and big game will be pushed around some more, and vacationers will be disappointed. The quality of life that species (including *Homo sapiens*) now enjoy in parklands will be adversely affected.

Hopefully the comebacks of ospreys, bald eagles, and peregrine falcons will not be in vain. Hopefully the recent chainsaw advertisement — "We came. We sawed. We conquered." — will not be taken seriously. We've come too far for that. Instead, Albert Schweitzer's comments should guide us through the Eighties and beyond. He said that we aren't truly civilized if we are concerned only with the relationship of man to man. What's really important is the relationship of man to all life on earth.

Bibliography

This bibliography is a list of the major sources which helped in the preparation of this guide. Anyone interested in reading more about birds of prey should consult any of the following books, which are arranged according to where they were used in the chapters.

Introductory Remarks (Raptors and Man)
Carson, Rachel. *Silent Spring.* Houghton Mifflin Co., Boston, 1962.

Halliday, Jack. *Vanishing Birds.* Holt, Rinehart and Winston, N.Y., 1978.

Harwood, Michael. *The View from Hawk Mountain.* Charles Scribner's Sons, N.Y., 1973.

Sparks, John, and Soper, Tony. *Owls: Their Natural and Unnatural History.* Taplinger Publishing Co., N.Y., 1970.

Tyler, Hamilton, and Phillips, Don. *Owls by Day and Night.* Naturegraph Publishers, Inc., Happy Camp, Ca., 1978.

Observation Guidelines (Identification)

Brett, James. *Feathers in the Wind*. Hawk Mountain Sanctuary Association, Kempton, Pa., 1973.

Brown, Vinson. *Knowing the Outdoors in the Dark*. Collier Books, N.Y., 1972.

Bull, John, and Farrand, John, Jr. *The Audubon Society Field Guide to North American Birds: Eastern Region*. Alfred A. Knopf, N.Y., 1977.

Collins, Henry Hill, Jr. *Complete Field Guide to American Wildlife*. Harper and Row, Publishers, Inc., N.Y., 1959.

Peterson, Roger Tory. *A Field Guide to the Birds*. Houghton Mifflin Co., Boston, 1980.

Robbins, Chandler S., Bruun, Bertel, and Zim, H.S. *Birds of North America*. Golden Press, N.Y., 1966.

Robinson, Leif, and Stymeist, Robert, eds. *Where to Find Birds in Eastern Massachusetts*. Bird Observer of Eastern Massachusetts, Inc., Belmont, Ma., 1978.

Natural History (Hunting and Nesting)

Bent, Arthur Cleveland. *Life Histories of North American Birds of Prey,* in two parts. Dover Publications, Inc., N.Y., 1961.

Chapman, Frank M. *Handbook of Birds of Eastern North America*. Dover Publications, Inc., N.Y., 1966.

Craighead, John J., and Craighead, Frank C., Jr. *Hawks, Owls, and Wildlife*. Dover Publications, Inc., N.Y., 1969.

Forbush, Edward Howe. *Birds of Massachusetts and other New England States*. Massachusetts Dept. of Agriculture, Norwood Press, 1927.

Harrison, Hal H. *A Field Guide to Birds' Nests*. Houghton Mifflin Co., Boston, 1975.

Pearson, T. Gilbert, ed. *Birds of America*. Doubleday and Co., Inc., N.Y., 1936.

Sprunt, Alexander, Jr. *North American Birds of Prey*. Harper and Bros., N.Y., 1955.

Stokes, Donald W. *A Guide to the Behavior of Common Birds*. Little, Brown and Co., Boston, 1979.